HelloToYourGreatnessTravel.com

Tired of Hearing Others Tell Their Exciting Vacation Stories?

Tell your own stories of a luxurious ocean cruise!
Cabo San Lucas, Mexico, November 6, 2008-November 10, 2008

Dr. Ida Greene, RTA, invites you to join her on a 4-day luxury vacation cruise on Carnival Elations to Cabo San Lucas, Mexico, the Jewel of the Baja. While enjoying the sun on this dream vacation, you will be able to **"Jump Into Your Greatness** with her uplifting, seminar on board. Arlyne Thompson, 3rd level Director will share, "How to Increase Your Profits." To reserve your spot call Dr. Ida Greene at 619-262-9951, or go to www.hellotoyourgreatnesstravel.com then click on Book Travel, Click on Group (top right) Scroll down to,

— BOOKS —
by Dr. IDA GREENE

Angels Among Us, Earth Angels

Have you met someone and it seems you knew them? Has a stranger come to your rescue at the right moment? Do you know someone who is like an Angel? There are seen and unseen Angels among us. Remember to speak or smile when someone does the same to you. It could be your Guardian Angel or an Earth Angel. ISBN-1-881165-20-5; $12.95

How to Be a Success in Business

This book helps you understand the business world and what is required for you to be a success in a business. It teaches you how to start, manage and grow a business successfully. ISBN-1-881165-03-5; $15.95

Say Goodbye to Your Smallness, Say Hello to Your Greatness

This book will help you understand why you say you want money, success, positive feelings, wealth and you never achieve it. It will raise your awareness and assist you in accepting your Greatness. ISBN-1-881165-07-8; $15.95

Money, How to Get It, How to Keep It

Most of us have negative mental programming surrounding money and money substance. This book helps you release your negative beliefs, thoughts and behaviors in relation to money. It

Secret of Success

Most people who become successful and wealthy know what is their life purpose and use that to create wealth. Success is an inside to outside spiritual un-foldment. When you connect your passion to the way you make money, you will have success. This book gives you tips on how to do that and enjoy the journey to success ISBN-1-881165-21-3, $15.95

How to Improve Self-Esteem in the African American Child

African American children struggle on a daily basis to live with and accept their skin color, their culture, and how to blend into society without losing themselves. The truth is we can bleach our skin; however we cannot make it black. All skin colors are beautiful, especially black. ISBN-1-881165-15-9, $15.95

Soft Power Skills, Women & Negotiation

This book focuses on the soft side of power and many women think of power and often respond in a manner as if they are afraid of power and the negotiation process. The basic premise is that negotiation is fun and is a learned behavior. It reminds you that everything is negotiable and shows you how to get your desires met through the negotiation process. Resolving conflict is easy and not to be feared. Order through www.authorhouse.com ISBN-1-41845568 $15.95

Anger Management Skills for Men

Are You feeling out of control and unable to express your feelings without "blowing your stack". You may be a habitual over-reactor. This book will give you the tools on how to deal with

SECRETS
of
SUCCESS

Ida Greene, Ph.D.

ATTENTION COLLEGES AND UNIVERSITIES, CORPORATIONS, AND PROFESSIONAL ORGANIZATIONS:
Quantity discounts are available on bulk purchases of this book for educational training purposes, fund raising, or gift giving. For information contact:
P. S. I. Publishers, 2910 Baily Ave. San Diego, CA 92105 (619) 262-9951.

ACKNOWLEDGEMENTS

I Wish To Thank The Following:

My mother who encouraged me to get an education, and my father who showed me how to be an entrepreneur, both are deceased.

In Pensacola, Florida where I grew up, I thank, my fifth and sixth grade teacher, Mrs. Bascom; my eighth grade teacher, Mrs. Ragland; tenth, eleventh and twelfth grade teacher; Mrs. E. B. Debose, all who saw my potential before I was aware of it.

My college advisor, Dr. I.N. McCollom, for helping me to stretch beyond my limitations to reach for higher goals, and to God for implanting within me a spirit of power, courage and a sound mind.

Ida Greene

Since the first publication of this book, I have established a non profit organization called, Our Place Center of Self-Esteem, which assists children, and families coping with issues of abuse. A portion of the sale from each book is donated to Our Place Center of Self-Esteem. Dr. Ida Greene, conducts seminars, and Coaches on personal/ professional development. Please call us at (877) 767-LOVE.

Other best-seller books by Dr. Ida Greene:
Light the Fire Within You
Are You Ready for Success
Self-Esteem, the Essence of You
Soft Power Negotiation Skills™
How to Be A Success In Business
Money, How to Get, How To Keep It
Angels Among Us, Earth Angels
Say Goodbye to Your Smallness, Say Hello to Your Greatness

CDs
Money, How to Get, How To Keep It
Light The Fire Within You
Say Goodbye to Your Smallness, Say Hello to Your Greatness

DVD
Soft Power Negotiation Skills

The Road to Success

I believe there is a natural impulse within all creation to evolve, expand and refine itself; we either stagnate and die or better ourselves and live, more productive and fuller lives. All of nature tells us to change and evolve; notice the leaves on a tree as they move from a flower blossom to a leaf, and the seasons of the year as they go from cool to warm and wet to dry. Nothing ever remains the same including our body which works continuously to digest, assimilate and maintain a state of normalcy regardless of the kinds of food we eat.

There is a peculiar characteristic about us humans that make us want to better our condition and improve our lifestyle. God has implanted within us a striving to be more, to strive for completion and wholeness; the foundation on which is self-esteem, self-confidence, and faith in a power greater than ourselves. Many of us seek to make changes in our outer lives yet fail to listen to our inner prompting. Yet there are others, who, only want to eat, sleep, and live a life of quiet desperation, futility, hopelessness, and helplessness. We were born to procreate and create, to improve our life and the lives of others through the accomplishment of our dreams and aspirations in life. When we become better, those around us become better also. Therefore, it is in the best interest of society, for all of us to want more out of life, to strive to improve our life and the lives of those around us. This is what success is all about. Success is the progressive realization of a worthwhile goal and the attainment of that goal. When we are actively pursuing a goal, it brings joy, hope and excitement into our lives. There is an exhilaration of love, compassion and understanding for others. It all begins with us helping us. However, we must feel worthwhile and deserving of something better in life for it to become a reality in our life. The road to success is beset with obstacles and seeming challenges. This is good, for it gives us an opportunity to employ the principles of faith, hope and confidence.

Maybe you are thinking that success is for a chosen few and you are not one of them. If this is your thinking, begin now to erase that idea from your mind. Success is a natural state of being for all. There are three types of success — personal, spiritual, and financial. You will need to decide what type of success is right for you at this point in your life. It may be personal success, where you work on your relationships with others; spiritual success, whereby you decide if there is a Supreme Power in the universe and discover your relationship to that power. On the other hand, you may need an improvement of your material success, so you can better provide for your family's daily needs or give more financially to your church or favorite charity. Whatever the reason, success awaits you; it is your natural heritage and right, to want more and to want to improve the lives of other.

This book explores the creative urge within each of us to procreate, create and improve our life and the lives of others through the accomplishment of our dreams and aspirations in life.

When we become better, those around us become better also. Therefore, it is in the best interest of society, for all of us to want more out of life, to strive to improve our life and the lives of those around us. This is what success is all about. Success is the progressive realization of a worthwhile goal and the attainment of that goal. When we are actively pursuing a goal, it brings joy, hope and excitement into our lives. There is an exhilaration of love, compassion and understanding for others. It all begins with us striving to better ourselves and improve our lives. we must feel worthwhile and deserving of something better in life for it to become a reality in our life. The road to success is beset with obstacles and seeming challenges. This is good, for it gives us an opportunity to employ the principles of faith, hope and confidence.

Maybe you are thinking that success is for a chosen few and you are not one of them. If this is your thinking, begin now to erase that idea from your mind. Success is a natural state of being for us all There are four types of success-Personal, Social, Spiritual, and Financial. You will need to decide what type of success is right for you at this point in your life. You will need to master all four before you achieve completion or make your transition from planet earth. So do not delay, start today. Success is your birthright.

INTRODUCTION

This book is dedicated to the entrepreneur, the future leader of tomorrow. The world desperately needs you. It needs your ingenuity, intuition, compassion, caring nature, love, and sense of justice. The world needs you to guide it, as mankind embarks on the age of high technology, space travel, and mass communication.

Entrepreneurship is increasing, however, men as well as women must work together to create a new world order, one that draws upon the strengths of both sexes to create a loving, caring, humane society where no one is inferior nor superior to another.

Many of us would rather do anything but improve our financial circumstances. There is a perception that to have money involves hard work and a denial of pleasure. What it will require is for you to take action to make your dreams becomes a reality. To experience more money or success in life, it will require you to: Increase your faith factor, have a strong belief in a divine benevolent power to sustain and support you, be willing to do all you are able to do, know when to let go so that God can guide you in the right direction, be open to miracles and know that there is nothing that God can't do. You must be willing to learn and grow emotionally, intellectually, and spiritually. Also you will need to change any negative mental programming you have about money and success. Say to your self right now "money is a tool I can use, to improve the quality of life for others and myself.".

CONTENTS

Chapter 1

SUCCESS, A HIGHER CALLING FOR LEADERSHIP

We are all light-bearers. We must all begin to let our light shine. We need to become people who display love, intuition, compassion, ingenuity, a caring nature, and a sense of justice. Both men and women must lead mankind to a new level of integrity, and personal interaction. Take with you on your success journey the weapons of compassion, honesty, justice, truth, faith, love, right action, and peace as you interact with other human beings at home and abroad.

It is time to take action. The world seeks your ideas and opinions. Believe in yourself. Believe in the goodness of all people. Seek to develop the best in yourself. Know that both women and men can be leaders. Now that you are in charge, expect to deal with criticism. As a leader you have to sacrifice being liked. Popularity sometimes suffers in the name of a job well done.

Choose today, to be a light leader. To be a leader of light demands you stay closely in touch with your inner spiritual self and blend it with your intellectual, social, and emotional self to become a new person. Become a person who is both human and divine; who operates from this premise continuously. Not everyone can be an enlightened leader, will you be the one? Are you ready for success?

There are many steps along the path to success. If your thoughts are infected with caution and doubt, your feelings will range from worry to fears. Some common fears you may experience are: Fear of achievement, fear of failure, fear of success, and low self-confidence.

Fear inhibits our efforts to achieve our desires and dreams. We want to achieve but, we hear a voice inside our head that says, "Can you do this?" If the answer inside of you says "I'm not sure," more than likely you will never achieve your dream without some Coaching to help you move through your self manufactured fears of success. Your dreams eventually fade away and die if they are not fueled with desire or expectation of accomplishment. Without ever knowing why, you begin to feel empty, hollow, lack energy, drive or enthusiasm. If this has happened to you, that is all right. You can start anew today. I hope this book will nudge you to get started and work through the barriers you have allowed to come between you, and the successful completion of your dreams and goals.

Success *means different things to different people.* Success to you may mean losing ten pounds of unwanted weight; to another individual who is a single parent it may mean making enough money to feed and clothe three children. Yet to another person it may mean making $100,000 a year. While to a home-maker whose children no longer need her, it may signal her transition into the work force for the first time to experience a different kind of success. To a woman it may mean finding work that will fill her inner needs for empowerment. Yet to a man, success has a different meaning if he sees himself as the provider of his family. What unfulfilled need/wants do you have, that are prodding you to do something different with your life? Why do you want to accomplish something? Whatever you define as success, it will entail that you take a risk. Success entails taking risks, ability to get things done, and the right uses of power.

My definition of success is the ability and willingness to take risks, to reach a goal or objective, and the ability to use power in a judicious manner.

Power or leadership is the ability to make a decision and follow through with it regardless of the consequences. Power is situational and is relative to the task before you. The kinds of power available to us and the way we use power, will vary depending upon the situation, circumstances, and perceived status of the person involved in the interaction. The key factor in the use of power is to act, or decide without hesitation.

Most people could benefit from a course in the uses of power and decision making. You will need these skills whether you desire success or not. Stop right now, Take a journey within. Then ask yourself, Am I ready for success? If you are ready for success, there are some basic fears you will need to overcome before you embark on your journey to success. The first fear is a Fear of Power.

Fear of Power is a major challenge for many women, because they have learned to associate power with the male gender. Therefore, when many women have a chance to use power, or are in a powerful position they emulate the male behavior, for that position. They fail to modify or feminize their position. So they become confused in their role identity and uncomfortable in their body; because of incongruence between what they are doing and how they perceive themselves. Power is situational. It is always affected by one's gender.

Power is not power if one does not have the ability to reinforce one's position of command, or if it is unheeded by those under its command. Most people respect authority and positions of authority. However, there are a few individuals who like to challenge authority figures. If you should ever find yourself in this position, you will need to confront the individual to resolve the matter swiftly and effectively. Otherwise, it can act as a smoldering flame, which if ignored will be to your disadvantage.

Power not used or misused is just a bad as no power at all. Power must be used in a judicious manner to serve and benefit all parties. The next fear to master is the fear of being different.

Fear of Being Different. This fear ties closely with a fear of power. To be a woman is to be different, just as it is different to be a man. It is great to be a woman, to be an African-American, to be An A Jewish, Japanese, Chinese, Asian, A Puerto Rican, short, tall, fat, skinny, to speak with an accent, etc. These are qualities that enhance our beauty and individuality. Others will only see these qualities as a problem if you do. Acknowledge that you are different, which is wonderful and get on with the tasks before you.

Fear of not Being Liked or Accepted is a problem only if you allow it to become one. The truth of the matter is that not everyone will like you. Many people hate themselves, so it stands to reason that they will hold you in the same esteem as they do themselves. Just accept that you will not please everyone, and that not all people will like you, for reasons only they know the answer. Just accept it as a fact of life and get on with the business of living your life from integrity and purpose. Seek to get people's respect, not their affection.

If people respect the decision you make, that is enough. The decision you make in their regard may not please them and that is o.k. You are not in a popularity contest to see how many people like or dislike you. You are in your job to reach the company' objectives and get your job done in the most judicious manner possible. Most times it is not what we say but the way in which we say something that creates conflict between us and others.

Most people can handle negative feedback, if it is given in a tactful manner and presented in the form of a sandwich. We sandwich our negative remarks between two positive statements. To try this, give the person one or two positive compliments, then share the negative feedback and remember to conclude with a positive statement. People always remember the last thing we say to them, so be sure to leave them with a positive image of the words you want them to maintain.

Leadership is a lot like fighting on a battlefield. Our personal interactions do not always turn out as we would like due to the individuality of others perception of our behavior. Our behavior may be interpreted by others as disapproval or acceptance. We may not always win all of the little battles of life. But, if we can leave others with peace in our minds and heart about our interaction with them commend yourself. For human nature does not always follow a prescribed course of action.

Fear of Disapproval/Rejection is related to the need to be liked. If you received a fair share of disapproval and or rejection by a parent figure, you may have a sensitivity towards this and you may wrongly interpret a "no" response and criticism as disapproval or rejection. It is wise not to be overly sensitive. As the saying goes, "Don't wear your heart on your sleeves." It is natural that not all people will agree with the ideas and opinions of all people. Isn't that great? The world would be boring without disagreements.

Fear of Failure – You may ask yourself, what if I fail? So what if you fall down and skin your knee? Do you stay down on the ground? No, you get up, brush yourself off and continue with your business. We must approach success with the same attitude. Success is not always a straightforward path. You may have to zigzag along the way. You may take a detour. Or, you may stop at any destination along the way and pause.

ASSESS YOUR LEADERSHIP ABILITY

Do you have what it takes to build an extraordinary career? This pop quiz will help you find out.

I have a clear understanding of what drives value in the marketplace for professional talent.
A. Strongly agree ☐   B. Neutral ☐   C. Strongly disagree ☐

I focus more actively on achieving personal career success than on helping my subordinates and peers become successful.
A. Strongly agree ☐   B. Neutral ☐   C. Strongly disagree ☐

I have trouble getting the job without the experience, and getting the experience without the job.
A. Strongly agree ☐   B. Neutral ☐   C. Strongly disagree ☐

When I have achieved my primary objectives, I am more likely to work to surpass them than to direct my attention to new, value-added activities.
A. Strongly agree ☐   B. Neutral ☐   C. Strongly disagree ☐

My current job fully utilizes my professional strengths and passions.
A. Strongly agree ☐   B. Neutral ☐   C. Strongly disagree ☐

How Do You Rate?
1. **Strongly agree**: Successful executive tend to have a deep understanding of the factors that influence their value in the marketplace- everything from demographic trends to the demand for various skills. They then act on that knowledge to help increase their values over time.
2. **Strongly disagree**: More than 90 percent of the most successful executives studied by Spencer Stuart focus at least as much on the success of those around them as on their own success. They do

not claw their way to the top, but in fact are carried there by sub-ordinates invested in their success. They create an environment that attracts tip talent and inspires exceptional performance.

3. **Strongly disagree**: This is the quintessential employment Catch 22 — you can't get the job without the experience, but you can't get the experience without the job. Without exception, however, the successful executives surveyed by Spencer Stuart overcame the paradox, either with career-defining accomplishments that marked them as all-around talents or with incremental advances that gradually broadened their range of skills.

4. **Strongly disagree**: Career top-performers don't just seek to exceed their predefined objectives. Instead, they storm past their assigned tasks to deliver unexpected, positive results that set them apart from their peers.

5. **Strongly agree**: Those achieving extraordinary success were over five times more likely than their peers to feel passionate about their jobs. Being fully engaged with your work is not a benefit of being successful-it's a prerequisite to getting there.

Chapter 2

DEVELOP YOUR INNER SELF TO ACHIEVE SUCCESS

Your self-esteem can support or destroy your capacity to make good choices and the choices you make can strengthen or lower your self-esteem. Self-esteem gives you the disposition to expect success from your efforts and know that you are worthy of success. It also allows you to accept your efforts when you produce something less than what you define as success, without experiencing self-degradation. Self-esteem gives you the confidence to get up and try again when you've had the wind kicked out of you. It gives you the option of trying something different than you have tried before, knowing that it may or may not result in your desired outcome.

Self-esteem is both the cause and effect of our leading inappropriate lives. When you have high self-esteem it allows you to try new things knowing that who you are does not affect the outcome. Your self-esteem is also intertwined with your personal integrity. Each time you act in accordance with your belief about who you are, you reinforce your decision that your belief is true. Likewise, when you have low self-esteem, your actions are often held back by your fear that you can't accomplish the deed in front of you. When you hold back, you reinforce your belief and prove yourself right.

Your subconscious mind will always create situations to prove itself right. If you think you can or can't do something, you're right. We only react to situations on which we already have a negative belief. The thing that can hurt you the most is holding negative thoughts about yourself.

If I said you were foolish for wearing those pink slippers, you might think I was crazy. However, if I said that those extra pounds that you've put on don't look too good on you, you might be hurt if you were self-conscious about your weight. The only thing in the above examples is that you would have a negative reaction in response to a negative thought that you already had about yourself.

When you can release all your negative self-talk, someone else's comments about who you are will no longer stay inside you. This is the attainment of mastery in self-esteem. Positive self-talk goes a long way to improve your self-esteem. Always concentrate on your successes rather than on what you feel are your failures. Be gentle with yourself and acknowledge what you are doing is right

This section will help you understand self-motivation, and what you must do on a daily basis to stay motivated. So you are able to face the barriers or fears that will surface to block your vitality and cause you to feel depressed, un-motivated, procrastinate and give up on your dreams. The key is an improved self-esteem, based on a new self-image you create.

Your self-esteem is endless, ongoing, and eternal. It is the essence, of who you are, not what you or others see you as. It is fragile, can be affected by many factors, and needs maintenance on a continual basis. The self-esteem you spend months to develop can be destroyed in one minute, by a careless remark, or unkind word. Our self-esteem is the vehicle that gets us to our chosen goals in life. However, the foundation and the fuel that propel us is our self-image and self-belief. Each time you change, you create a new you. So your self-image needs to match the new role you will play. You will never be congruent, until the "play you," matches the real you. The things all people need whether or not they want success in their career are:

1. **Security** – Safety
2. **Self-Esteem** – Is a process where you are esteemed and made to feel that you count, that you make a difference by your presence in the family unit. Identification
3. **Self-Worth** – Your value to family and to yourself
4. Acceptance – Self-appreciation.

Affirm for yourself:

I acknowledge the divine , glorious, magnificent person that I am. Since I am made in the image, and likeness of God, I allow this unlimited power to guide and direct my life. I give up all sense of smallness to express my divine unlimited potential.

To Develop Your Inner Self, Ask Yourself These Questions
1. Who Am I? I am:

2. Finish this Sentence:
    "I am a product of my upbringing because".:

3. What I Want From Life Is:

4. a) My Likes Are:

    b) My Dislikes Are:

5. I Am Good At Doing:

6. Finish this statement,
    If I could only do one kind of work in life, it would be…

Start now and enjoy the rest of your life. *Life Is Shorter Than You Think.*

DESIDERATA

Go placidly amid the noise and the haste and remember what peace there may be in silence. As far as possible without surrender, be on good terms with all people. Speak your truth quietly and clearly; and listen to others, even to the dull and ignorant; they too have their story. Avoid loud and aggressive persons; they are vexatious to the spirit. If you compare yourself with others, you may become vain or bitter, for always there will be greater or lesser persons than yourself.

Enjoy your achievements as well as your plans. Keep interested in your own career, however humble; it is a real possession in the changing fortunes of time. Exercise caution in your business affairs, for the world is full of trickery. But let this not blind you to what virtue there is ; many persons strive for high ideals, and everywhere life is full of heroism. Be yourself. Especially do not feign affection. Neither be cynical about love; for in the face of all aridity and disenchantment, it is as perennial as the grass.

Take kindly the counsel of the years, gracefully surrendering the things of youth. Nurture strength of spirit to shield you in sudden misfortune. But do not distress yourself with dark imaginings. Many fears are borne of fatigue and loneliness. Beyond a wholesome discipline, be gentle with yourself. You are a child of the Universe no less than the trees and the stars; you have a right to be here. And whether or not it is clear to you, no doubt the universe is unfolding as it should.

Therefore, be at peace with God, whatever you conceive him to be, and whatever your labors and aspirations in the noisy confusion of life, keep peace in your soul. With all its sham drudgery, and broken dreams, it is still a beautiful world.

Be cheerful. Strive to be happy.

I AM WORTH IT

I may sometime cause confusion when I am unclear in my communication, unsure of myself, or uncertain about an outcome, yet I am worth the bother.

I may act timid and fearful sometimes, but please remember that I am trying to sort things out in my mind, and I am worth the bother.

Even though you may struggle to understand me, I am worth it.

My friend, I am the other half of you.

I am incomplete without you, and you are incomplete without me.

In some strange way, though we differ in racial composition, thoughts, ideas, and behavior; we are wedded to each other.

I will release you for now, to soar above the heavens. Just remember that whatever disappointment or challenge I face,

I deserve the best, for I am worth it.

— IDA GREENE

If you believe in yourself and believe in a power greater than yourself, you will achieve success. Since the largest growing population in the United States today is the 85 years and older group, you will journey many times in your lifetime from success to success before you make your transition from planet earth. Often success is the result of patient persistence through failure. So do not become discouraged if you do not see instant results.

We are all a diamond in the rough, becoming our Christ-Self through our trials and tribulations. Jesus stated "Be of good cheer, for

12

I have conquered the world." You must never quit striving to improve yourself, or your life circumstances, even though you may have challenges, and it takes a long time to reach your goals.

Your success is created from your self expression. And your self-expression is a spiritual quality. You are here in life to express your Divine potential. Do not confuse your Divine self expression with your livelihood. When you allow God to express through you, all your needs will be met. Never accept a job, or engage in any activity just for money. If you do not express your divine, God given talents, you will become disgruntled, bored, and lose enthusiasm for life and living. And when you lose your enthusiasm, you lose your light. Jesus said, "You are the light of the world." You are alive, joyous, and aglow when you do work you enjoy, and it fulfills a divine purpose in the universe.

You are a spiritual being, in a human body, having a spiritual experience. Your primary purpose to be on the planet is to use your divine self expression to grow spiritually, and become a Master like Jesus. We must first master our physical body, before we achieve mastery in our spiritual life. And we do this through right thinking, right living, and right self expression. Success is not just about desire, power, and money. It is a spiritual and sacred journey.

Both life and success are about your journey, learned experiences, and personal growth. We grow through each challenge we encounter. No challenge you experience in life will ever leave you where it found you. Every experience you have teaches you how to be more humble, gentle, loving, compassionate, and how to forgive seventy times seventy. You are here in this life to become your Divine-Self. We become our Divine Self by listening and responding to the intuition God gives us. It is designed to bring forth the Divine and best aspect of our nature so we become God in human form.

13

We came from God, and to God we return when we complete our earths' journey. Remember, what you are, is Gods' gift to you. What you make of yourself is your gift to God. Will you return to God the same raw materials given you on your entrance to planet earth; or will you return to God a grand masterpiece. A work of art so magnificent to behold, that all the celestial angels take a bow. Because in everything you attempted, you put forth your best effort. You used your work, creativity, talents, relationships, friendships and painful life experiences to reach a higher level of service to your fellow man.

We were created to serve and be of service to God through our service to our fellow man. We serve God whenever we serve our fellow man. When we let go our pride, our prejudice, our possessions, our envy, our jealousy, our hurt feelings, our anger, and our ego; we take on angelic qualities. We become God in the flesh.

You were given dreams, goals, and aspirations to refine your temperament, your spirit, attitude, and to become more loving. Whenever you accomplish any goal, you set out to do, and accomplish it in spite of hardship, or challenge you are a success.

What is success for you, may not be success for another. God speaks to each of us individually. We are each marching to a different drummer.

Success is an inside job. You must first create it within your mind, before it will out picture in the real world of manifestation. And to create it in your mind you must do two things:
1. You must be willing to do whatever is necessary to heal yourself of a belief in a separation between you and God and a separation between you and others. The universal goal is for us to see ourselves as one. We were all created by one life force. There is one energy source, one life and one Divine Mind, that unites us as

14

people. We all tap into the same energy source to create prosperity, or anything we desire to have. The process is: Thought (ideas) lead to feelings, feelings leads to action; and, your actions create something tangible like writing, (taking a purchase order) talking, (coaching/counseling) or working to put in a television cable or working in the stock market.

2. To acquire wealth, or be successful, you must become a large channel for God to pour through you out into the universe. Your goal is to discover your talent and find a way to give your gift to the world. Reverend Margaret Wright feels the key to prosperity and abundance is in your giving. She says, "**The more you give, the more you get,**" so give of your time, talent, and treasure." And be more of a person that someone would want to be with in a business relationship."

Never compare your success or achievements with any other person. Only God alone is the judge, not you or another. For just when you think you have failed, God says, well done my good and faithful servant, you have fought a good fight. You are a success.

The tool you will need to achieve success in anything will be a positive self-esteem anchored in faith. Faith is a positive, mental state of knowing, that even though the outcome may be bleak, look hopeless, and impossible, that the perfect outcome you desire will manifest. Faith is the space where you let go, and grab onto the unknown. With faith you have to believe, and know, before what you want is manifested. Faith is letting Go and letting God take over. The human mind wants to know the outcome before it happens, because we like to be in control of things. If control is your issue, you will have little faith, abundance, prosperity, wealth, or success. Faith is about being out of control. It is letting go your control, to discover new horizons, and vistas. It is about gratitude. What can you be thankful for today. The following exercise can help you develop a more positive attitude.

15

One of the foundations for success is think positive thoughts and say positive affirmation like:

I feel good when I think about _____

Say To yourself and affirm:
Today I start a new day, a new month, a new year and I am a new person. I accept that I am success that I am successful in all I do, or will become.

Excellence Has No Fear Of Observation
Therefore when you are being your best, it does not matter if others watch you.

The 4-Way Test of what you think, say or do, is to ask yourself:
1. Is it the TRUTH?
2. Is it FAIR to all Concerned?
3. Will it Build GOODWILL and Better Friendships?
4. Will it Be BENEFICIAL to All Concerned?

If your answer is *yes* to all the above, you will be a huge success in your chosen endeavor.

RESPONSIBILITY
1. Responsibility means accepting the importance of the job we do. Work that we value is the only work that is valuable.
2. Responsibility means seeing things from a point-of-view big enough to include the people and the organization around us.
3. Responsibility means taking criticism as it is intended: an attempt to improve the quality of our efforts, without ridiculing us as people.
4. Responsibility means accepting the little, essential disciplines that go with any team operation – punctuality, neatness safety.
5. Responsibility means realizing that the situation at work is like

the situation at home – every single thing we do affects someone else, for better or worse.

6. Responsibility means accepting problems and difficulties as a normal part of any job. If we had no problems, we would win no victories, and without victories, life would be pretty drab.

7. Responsibility means looking at your complaints to see if they have solutions, or if you're just complaining about things that can't possibly be changed. Complain to someone who can do something to effect the change you want; back room complaints only make everyone unhappy. Be constructive — identify what you see as needing change, and then give positive suggestions about how you think changes can be made.

– Anon

Personal Success Inventory
Develop Your Strengths And Improve Your Weakness

Check the words that are true for you, circle ones you need to improve.

Confident	Angry
Superior	Shy
Handsome	Inferior
Sensitive	Planner
Thoughtful	Secure
Pleasant	Resourceful
Kind	Argumentative
Scared	Bold
Unfriendly	Competent
Controlling	Punctual
Bossy	Smart
Creative	Selfish
Giver	Joyful
Insecure	Friendly
Organized	Stingy

Chapter 3

FOLLOW YOUR BLISS

Success is not a something-for-nothing activity. Nothing in life is free. You will have to pay a price for everything you get in life including success. If you do nothing, nor aspire for anything in life; you will be one of a person who has no control over his or her destiny. You will be at the mercy of others; and looks to others to provide for and supply your daily needs. God gave us dominion over the earth. You cannot take dominion from a lowered mind-set. You must take a positive step up in your thinking and elevate your thoughts on a higher plane, so you are on a level with the greater good you seek. All good things in life are created from a divine, state of mind.

All things must be created through our cooperation with God, the union of our mind with the Supreme mind and subordinate our will to the will of God. The only power you and I have is the power we use, through the Divine mind. We, humans cannot create anything. We can be co-creators with God, if we understand and use the tools of spiritual intuition, reverence, and humble ourselves this Higher Power.

We are God's creation. We came from God therefore we are one with God. Just as an egg is a part of a chicken, we likewise are a part of God. We are the human manifestation of God. Everything that has breath is under the ruler ship of this "Supreme Power and Force," and stands obedient to this "Force," I refer, to, as God. The Universe is eternal and lives throughout all generations. If you live in obedience to the Divine laws of the universe and work within them you can create wonders. You will have many growth experiences until you learn when to push, when to pull and when to let go and allow God to take charge. To surrender and allow for divine intervention is one of the hardest lessons to learn. The lessons we have to learn and understand is there are two phases to the manifestation of what we desire. One is the active, doing phase and the other is the surrender and allowing phase. We have to take the time to prepare our mind and heart to develop a vision for what we want, become passionate about our dream and accept that it is on its way to us. God wants us to succeed, be successful and make a lot of money, because we can help a lot of people who are less fortunate than us We can have all the desires of our heart as long as we do not take from the good of another, and what we create, benefits others as well as ourselves.

If we have faith and look to God as the supplier of our ideas, desires, and aspirations we can have all we want, and more however we should never make a God of, or worship our possessions. *We come into this life with nothing, and we depart with nothing.*

All that we accumulate on our journey through life: Our experiences, memories, emotional growth, and our spiritual enlightenment help us to complete our spiritual growth and end our birth to death cycle. It s through our desires and goals we become motivated to change the circumstances in our life. Everything we achieve in life begins with a desire to excel and achieve. Our desire/s is an idea. An idea is a thought or a group of thoughts. It is an image or a picture in your mind. Napoleon Hill stated in the book *Think and Grow Rich*, "whatever the mind can conceive and believe it will achieve."

When you make a decision to have or create your thoughts/desires it then becomes a goal. All goals can be achieved through a plan of action. This plan of action is what I call success. Success is anything you desire to have, be or want to do. The following diagram shows you what you need to do to achieve success.

Desire to Excel →Goal Directness →Energy/Vitality →Enthusiasm →Fire/Light →Joy, Happiness, Love = Aliveness

Answer the questions below to help prepare you to be open to new ideas and opportunities for success:

1. Are you currently doing the kind of work that adds pleasure to your life, or are you bored and stuck into survival issues to earn a living or prepare for your future?

2. What goal(s) would give you energy, drive or desire to achieve?

3. What do you need to do to create a sense of urgency, to take a new path in life or work on a new goal?

4. If there were no barriers in your life, what would you be, do, or have? Where would you live? Let yourself daydream for a moment before you write your answers.

Basic Truths About Success

*Our word does not have to act, it is acted upon. Therefore it is
our business to know the Truth, and the Truth's business is
to produce the result.*
— ERNEST HOLMES

*He who binds himself to a Joy Doth the winged life destroy; but he
who kisses the Joy as it flies Lives in Eternity's sunrise.*
— WILLIAM BLAKE

COMMITMENT

Until one is committed there is hesitancy,
The chance to draw back, always ineffectiveness.
Concerning all acts of initiative
And creating there is one elementary truth,
The ignorance of which kills countless ideas
And splendid plans;
The moment one definitely commits oneself,
All sorts of things begin to happen that would
 never otherwise have occurred.
A whole stream of events issues from
The committed decision,
Raising in one's favor all matter of incidents,
Meetings and material assistance,
Which no (wo)man could have dreamed
Would come his/her way.
Whatever you can do, or dream you can do, begin it.
Boldness has genius, power and magic in it.
— GOETHE

The Top 10 Ways To Surrender To The Flow

THOMAS J. LEONARD.

1. Understand that there IS a flow and that it's bigger than you.
2. When facing a problem, seek to solve it immediately, taking the path of least resistance.
3. You don't know what you don't know, but that the flow does. Trust it.
4. The Universe never lies. If something is "off," so are you.
5. Seek to understand your environment (and personal relationships) and their affect on you.
6. Your body often knows more than you mind; Listen to your heart if you're not sure what to do.
7. There is an ebb and flow; if in doubt sometimes it's wise to do nothing.
8. The flow changes so you'll need to adapt to IT.
9. You affect the flow around you, even though the flow around you is bigger than you.
10. You want to BECOME the flow, not just be carried along BY the flow.

TEST YOUR SUCCESS POTENTIAL

1. Although I think a lot about success, I don't think I will totally succeed. True☐ False☐

2. I find it necessary to exaggerate about my performance in order to let people know my strengths, or how good I am. Frequently☐ Sometimes☐ Never☐

3. It is possible for me to be successful in One☐ Some☐ All areas of my life☐.

4. Although, I am content with my life, I am liable to find myself thinking about what someone else has achieved.
    Often☐   Sometimes☐   Never☐

5. I equate success with money and/or power.
    Yes☐   Partially☐   No☐

6. I have written goals for myself. Yes☐ No☐

7. I consistently evaluate myself. Yes☐ No☐

8. I have enough self-discipline to reorganize and redirect, if I find myself getting off track. Yes☐ No☐

9. I find myself thinking more about what success is than how I will get there. Always☐ Sometimes☐ No☐

10. My potential to succeed is a reality. I am where I want to be
    True☐   False☐

ARE YOU READY FOR SUCCESS TODAY

What you are is God's gift to you. What you make of yourself is your gift to God. On the basis of this premise answer the following question below. Write whatever comes to your mind, do not write what you think someone wants you to say or what you think God wants you to say or to do. Write a brief sentence for each question. Write quickly, do not contemplate whether your answers are right or wrong.

1. What does success mean to you?

2. What is your earliest memory of wanting to achieve or accomplish?

3. Who are your role models or whom do you admire?

4. What would you like to do, become, or have?

5. What would it take for you to be happy in life?

6. Define happiness for you.

7. Since we were created to be goal striving, achieving human beings, what contribution will you make for the betterment of mankind before you die?

8. Sit down in a quiet place close your eyes and go over the same questions in your mind. And again write whatever comes to mind.

To determine your quality/degree of life, answer the following questions to help you diagnose where you are on the continuum of birth → life → death, or life → life cycle.

1. Do you have a dream, or longing, you would like to achieve?

   What is it?

2. Is this a wish or a longing?

3. What is the difference to you between a wish, dream or longing/goal?

4. How will you decide what you really want out of life?

5. How do/will you decide between conflicting goals/dreams?

6. Has anyone in your family ever set a goal/s to do something, and accomplished it?

7. If your answer to the above is no, how will you develop a desire to achieve, or complete a goal if no one in your family has done the process to make a wish, or dream be a reality?

8. How will you acquire a drive to achieve your goal/s?

9. What aspect of your character will you need to develop that may be dormant or non existent? e.g. achiever, positive outlook, faith, stick-to-itness, motivation, drive etc.

10. Is the amount of money you make your indicator of success? If not what is your indicator of successful completion of a goal/success?

11. Do you feel it is unchristian to desire success, be successful, or have money?

12. Do you feel money is the "root of all evil," or the evil use of money is the "root of evil"?

13. Have you decided what you really want out of life or is what you want someone else's idea of what would be best for you to do?

14. How long will it take you to complete your goal/s or obtain your desired success?

15. Have you figured out how to start, so your goal becomes real?

a. **What is the first thing you will do to get started?** List each step of your plan, from step 1 to step 5. Write down now what you will do and how you will proceed. E.g. Decide on a short term goal I can complete in 30 days. These are the thing I will do to make my dream a reality. *I will do the following:*
   1. I will –

   2. I will –

b. Now go through the same process for your intermediate goal/s (90 days to 1 year.)
   1. I will –

   2. I will –

c. Now go through the same process for your long range goal/s (5–10 years).
   1. I will –

2. I will –

16.   How will you stay focused on your dream/goal?

17.   How will you handle setbacks or disappointment?

God does not cause bad things to happen to us. God works through us by changing our consciousness (mind set), and our heart. God never does anything to us or for us. We create our hardships, disappointments and bad luck through our negative thought patterns and our lack of faith that the perfect solution is emerging even though it may not be clearly evident to us at the time. It has been my experience that God reveals things to us in stages. Maybe it is because we need to develop the belief and acceptance or maybe we need time to prepare ourselves to receive the good He has in store for us. I used to get very impatient because it seemed to take God a long time to give me what I had requested. Now I realize that my doubts and negative thinking acted as a hindrance to my positive expectation. God wants us to show gratitude and thankfulness for what he will do for us before he does it. I thought I would give gratitude and thanks after the facts like with my parents, however God works differently from our human parents. I have to remind myself what my mother always said. She said God said "If you take one step, I will take two".Which means we have to take action first to show God that we are serious and he will help us complete the task

WORDS OF WISDOM
The great end of life is not knowledge, but action.
— THOMAS HENRY HUXLEY

They that seek the Lord shall not want any good thing
— PSALM 34:10

Every moment you continue to hold back and hide your divinity, power and love, you live in the halls of mediocrity. The person who Dare to be alive has the courage and willingness to fail, to look foolish, to risk embarrassment or have others think what they may about them.

It requires unusual courage to dare to be fully alive in a world where everyone is living a careful life and trying not to disturb the status quo, passively hoping for the best, desperately trying to outwit disease and death. Do you have the courage to be "fully" alive?

Can you being a Zorba, Rockefeller, or Einstein? Who will be leaping onto the table top, wildly spinning and offering heart and soul to live a life of fullness and love? Who will be the great celebrated singers, dancers, poets, laughers, and lovers? Who among you will refuse to buy into the conspiracy of this world that asks us to play small? I dare you to take a stand for love in this life and allow your own particular creative expression to flow through you. Despite the seeming fear of danger of doing so, the instant you make a leap of faith, you join the ranks of greatness. Those who dare to be fully alive in the midst of all that is taking place in the world. I ask who among you will be great, If not you, then who?

POSITIVE THOUGHTS
The trouble is, if you don't risk anything, you risk even more.
— ERICA JONG

I discovered I always have choices and sometimes it's only a choice of attitude. — ABRAHAM LINCOLN

Follow your bliss and what look like walls will turn into doors
— JOSEPH CAMPBELL, Mythologist and folklorist

One does what one is; one becomes what one does.
— ROBERT ELDLER VON MUSIL Novelist and essayist

What is it that you want to do that would captivate your heart, make you feel alive, so in love with your work or livelihood that it seems to you like "play".And you wonder why they are paying you to have fun. What goal or objective would you like to achieve? It is time to take those old dreams out of the closet. It is time to daydream again. Just as you did when you were a child. Remember when you believed in magic? You thought it, believed it, and it happened. You were blissful.

Let's pretend again. It is time to let yourself digress back in time to age 4, or 5, the age of magic. Somewhere between the ages of two and nine, magical things seemed to happen all the time. Find a quiet place where you will not be disturbed and close your eyes. Sit an erect position. Breathe in and exhale two times. Let's take a journey back in time, in your memory, to a time where you believed in magic; when you did not have: a fear of power, a fear of success, fear of failure, fear of identity loss, fear of having too much money, fear of not having enough money, fear of being different, fear of disapproval, nor did you have a fear of being disliked or accepted. Allow yourself to bask in this state for 15 minutes or more. If an angel or fairy god mother shows up or a holy being, allow them to talk to you or take you on a magical journey. When you open your eyes, write in your journal or note book any new words of wisdom given to you. review this information daily for seven days then weekly for one month. Try to incorporate this information into your business as appropriate.

What happened between the age of nine and your mid-twenties? Who stole your dreams? Who told you that your ideas were foolish, that they could never happen, and even more importantly, you could not accomplish your "far-out" dreams? Was it an over cautious parent, or someone who feared you might experience rejection or ridicule? Was it a shortsighted friend or acquaintance? Did you think that the mind stopped growing with the body? Who taught you how to be so cautious? Dreams are the healthy infants, who live inside us, and if properly nurtured with desire, develop into a passion for achievement, and success. We feel full of bliss and is in love with life and living.

To Discover Your Passion, Ask Yourself These Questions:

1. What things in life give me the greatest pleasure and satisfaction? Write these down as now. Select one area that brings you the greatest joy and sense of fulfillment, and write about it

    Personal:

    Professional:

Social:

Spiritual:

2. What things do others praise or compliment you on? Do you agree with them? Are you currently doing this type of work? If your answer is "no", Why?

List ways you can develop skills in these area/s.

GOALS AND OUTCOMES

In order for you to get the maximum benefit, list four goals or outcomes you want to change, improve or develop in your business. *Outcome* – (Be as specific as possible)

_____

_____

_____

_____

_____

_____

List three reasons why it is important for you to achieve this goal.

1. _____

2. _____
   _____

3. _____
   _____

State how you would feel right now if this was true and you had reached your goal.

Start with a dream that is personal and small, but worth doing. Then dream a bigger dream. Keep dreaming until your dreams seem impossible to achieve. Then you'll know you're on the right track. Then you'll know you're ready to conjure up a dream big enough to define your future and perhaps your generation's future.
                    – VANCE GOFFMAN, Business executive

Live the Fullness of Life, Now

It is a deep satisfaction to be alive today. I am glad I know who I am and what I am. I am a child of God. It is satisfying to know that everything I do is the action of God within me. I experience the full gratification of every desire, when I make my will one with the Universal will. God working within me satisfies my every demand on the eternal law of perfect self expression. I live at the point of cause, and the effect is complete fulfillment.

My life is the Father's life and is an outlet for his creativity to express through me. I am the focal point in the universal creative mind of God. I am a willing servant, and open vessel for the Goodness of God to flow through, and so it is.

When you cannot get a compliment in any other way,
pay yourself one.– MARK TWAIN

Whatever you do or dream you can do, begin it.
Boldness has genius, power, and magic in it.
– GOETHE

If You Can Imagine It, You Can Achieve It,
If You Can Dream It, You Can Become It.
– KRISTONE

HOW TO VISUALIZE WHAT YOU WANT

There are many books written about visualization. Here is an easy and simple way to utilize visualization techniques to accomplish the things you desire in life. The objective is to use your imagination to conjure a picture in your mind's eye. Go ahead and try this now. This will work even if you are not a visual person. First gather all your supplies. You will need a red object. It can be an apple, a red piece of cloth, or an orange object. It can be a shoe, a blouse or a towel. Now let's begin. Become quiet and think about what you want to do. Stare at the red object for approximately 30 seconds. Now close your eyelids. Use your skills of imagery to see if you can picture a visual image of the red object flashing across the screen of your mind. If you can't, continue to practice in this manner until you can see a red object flashing across the screen in your mind's eye. It is O.K. to open your eyes to get a quick peek if the color begins to fade. Do this exercise once a day for one week. If you need more time, continue to practice this technique.

After you have mastered this, begin to associate anger, with the red color. Next practice this with the color yellow. Follow the same procedure with the yellow color, except associate the color yellow with the sunshine. Then think of the sunshine and associate the yel-

34

low color with happiness.

Now move to the next step of the visualization process. Begin to associate happiness with your new job, promotion, or goals you have outlined for your career. Now get a global picture in your mind's eye about the next step you need to take to move up the career ladder. Now see yourself in a new job position. Become very specific and detailed about what your new job will entail; the location or address of the building, the color of the building and the room.

Imagine the floor in the building where you will be working. Is it on the first floor or the tenth floor over looking the bay? See your name plate with the title on your desk. Imagine the color of the suit you will have on when you go for your interview at the corporation. See the Executive Manager, welcoming you into the firm, telling you that your salary is exactly what you had envisioned. If you leave out any details, go back over this guideline again. Continue daily to do this exercise until every objective you desire is accomplished.

If you are a doubtful person, who tends to imagine the worst outcome of everything, it will take a little longer for you to see positive results. This is a four-stage process.

First, you have to visualize what you want.
Second, you have to believe it can happen.
Third, you have to believe it can happen to you.
Fourth, you must believe you are deserving of this good.

There is a list of books and an audio cassette tape album in the back of this book that you can order to guide you through this process. Be persistent. Know that other people have reached their goals and why not you? Success is not a destination. It is a journey. The journey you will travel, as you achieve your dreams and goals. The following poem summarizes success.

35

You Must Not Quit

When Things Go Wrong As They Sometimes Will,
*   When The Road You're Trudging Seems All Uphill,*
When The Funds Are Low And The Debts Are High,
*   And You Want To Smile, But You Have To Sigh,*
When Care Is Pressing You Down A Bit......
*   Rest If You Must, But Do Not Quit.*
Life Is Queer With It's Twists And Turns,
*   As Everyone Of Us Sometimes Learns,*
And Many A Fellow Turns About
*   When They Might Have Won Had They Stuck It Out.*
Don't Give Up Though The Pace Seems Slow...
*   You Might Succeed With Another Blow.*
Often The Goal Is Nearer Than It Seems
*   To A Faint And Faltering Person;*
Often The Struggler Has Given Up
*   When They Might Have Won The Victor's Cup;*
And They Learned Too Late When the Night Came Down, How
*   Close They Were To The Golden Crown.*
Success Is Failure Turned Inside Out,
*   The Silver Tint Of The Clouds Of Doubt,*
And You Never Can Tell How Close You Are,
*   It May Be Near When It Seems Afar;*
So Stick to The Fight When You Are Hardest Hit,
*   It's When Things Seem Worst That You Must Not Quit.*

*   – A*NON

You are where you are today because of the thoughts you have entertained, every moment of the day. The mental images (visualization) you hold about yourself, your life, the expectations you have about your abilities, and the vision you entertain about your life's purpose. Reverend Michael Beckwith, who is featured in the movie, "The Secret" says visioning is different from visualization. He

36

describes it as a transformation of the human self, into the divine, spiritual self to allow the presence of God to use you. You do not tell God what to do, nor ask God for anything. You glorify God, by allowing God to express through you, for a "Higher" purpose to serve your fellow man. I suggest you start with visualization, to train your mind to mentally see what you desire and progress to the visioning process, as outlined by Michael Beckwith, where you become a master like the great mystics. And allow God to use you, by aligning yourself with divine ideas of joy, harmony, love, and wisdom. To do this you will need self-awareness.

Self-Awareness – Is the ability to see yourself as you really are, to accurately assess your own needs, your strong and weak points and areas in which you need to improve. It is easy to think that we are perfect and everyone else needs to improve. We can all become better people. Periodically make out a personal growth chart for yourself, grade yourself on a scale of one to ten. Some of the categories might be "quick temper," "easy going," "hard driver," "relaxed," "cooperative," "stubborn." Do this annually to gauge how much growth you have achieved. For greater effectiveness and to increase your self-awareness have a co-worker and a friend, grade you. Then compare the score you gave yourself to the score that each of them gave you.

IT'S A SPECIAL DAY

Something is occurring, something new is stirring. Something of the Spirit, blesses me today. Energies are swarming, totally transforming. Something of the Spirit blesses me with light.

Knowledge is provided, I am being guided. Something of the Spirit blesses me with light. I have perfect leading to the good I'm seeking. Something of the Spirit blesses me with light.

I accept my blessing; through it I'm expressing something of the Spirit Gloriously good. Every trouble ceases; all my joy increases. Something of the Spirit blesses me with good.

It's a special day, Its a special day. I can feel it deeply in a special way. It's a special day, it's a special day. I can feel it deeply in a special way.

          – WARREN MEYER and GEORGE A. MINOR

Maya Angelou said:

I've learned that no matter what happens, or how bad it seems today, life does go on, and it will be better tomorrow.

I've learned that you can tell a lot about a person by the way he/she handles these three things: a rainy day, lost luggage, and tangled Christmas tree lights.

I've learned that regardless of your relationship with your parents, you'll miss them when they're gone from your life.

I've learned that making a 'living' is not the same thing as 'making a life'.

I've learned that life sometimes gives you a second chance.

I've learned that you shouldn't go through life with a catcher's mitt on both hands; you need to be able to throw some things back.

I've learned that whenever I decide something with an open heart, I usually make the right decision.

I've learned that even when I have pains, I don't have to be one.

I've learned that every day you should reach out and touch someone. People love a warm hug, or just a friendly pat on the back.

I've learned that I still have a lot to learn.

I've learned that people will forget what you said, people will forget what you did, but people will never forget how you made them feel.

Chapter 4

Are You Ready for Financial Success?

Breaking Through Blocks to Money and Wealth

Money is one of the tools society says we need to feel successful or be a success in life. What are your thoughts about money? Do you feel money is blocking your being a success or feeling like you are a success? What do you feel is blocking the flow of money in your business or into your life?

Success is not measured by what a man or woman accomplishes, but by the opposition he or she overcame to reach their goals. You can be a success in any business you desire. The Reverend Johnnie Coleman, Pastor of the Christ Universal Complex in Chicago teaches, "You don't have to be sick or broke. You can go within and bring forth the power to change things." Each of us has within us a sleeping giant, which when activated with desire, a strong determination, and unrelenting persistence will eventually melt away the greatest obstacles in our path. Success, whether business or otherwise belongs to the person who will pursue what they desire tenaciously without giving in to despair, set backs, disappointment, tragedy or failure. They achieve success because they never look back with regret at the past, but continue to look ahead to the possibilities of the future. These people have an unshakable faith, and belief in a God that is ready, willing, and able to take care of them, and sustain them through their trials and tribulations.

Dr. Hugh Gloster, the past president of Morehouse College, when asked "what made him one of America's one hundred best college presidents? Replied, "You must establish your dreams and quietly move in the direction of attaining them." Much of this has to do with the way we use our mind. In the books, Working With The Law," by Raymond Holliwell and "Think And Grow Rich, A Black Choice," by Dennis Kimbro and Napoleon Hill, both authors discuss mental laws and how our use of them can create wealth.

Money is magnetic energy. You are a magnet attracting to you all things, through the signal you are emitting through your thoughts and feelings. Learn how to become a magnet for the creation of personal wealth by monitoring the thoughts you thinks for five minutes every hour for one day. Everything you see now began as an idea in some-one's mind. Your physical world is nothing more than the lingering evidence of that which has already taken place in your mind. It is an extension or out picturing of your thoughts. We live in a mental world. Raymond Holliwell states that, mental laws are the infrastruc-tures of life. Dr Dennis Kimbro states, "Just as one is blinded to phys-ical laws, mental laws are also undetectable to the eye." Your thoughts and ideas are living, breathing, things. They are the raw materials from which all that you desire, create or accomplish in life comes from.

Right now you are where you are in your business or financial condition because of the thoughts you are thinking. If you desire a change in your business or in your finances, you must examine the quality of the thoughts you entertain on an hourly basis. The more you think about lack, bad times, or scarcity, the more these circum-stances will appear in your life. William James, the Harvard Psychologist said, "You are what you think about most of the time." What you think increases and grows in proportion to the amount of energy thought you feed it. Therefore, if you desire success or wealth, make this your predominant thought for twenty-two hours in a twen-ty-four-hour day.

To have money or acquire money, will require you to increase your prosperity consciousness. And here are some principles that can help you. First, prosperity is a state of mind. As you think, you become. Second, prosperity is a state of mind that results from prosperous thoughts. It is the result of your recognition of your Divine self. Your inner self is a creative individual expression of God. Because the nature of God is abundant, and prosperous, when you identify your human nature with the Universe, you become an individualized, creative, expression of the universal mind of God. You were made in the image and likeness of God. Also you came from God and after your stay on earth you return to God. You are the vessel through which God manifest and express. So if the nature of God is prosperous, abundance, wholeness, perfection, and complete, then so are you.

You are not lacking in anything for the prosperity, abundance, and perfection of God to express through you. What is needed is a correction in your thinking and thought patterns. You need to make a shift in your mind set from lack to abundance, from helpless to hopeful, and from an impoverished outlook to a prosperous outlook. Learn to think optimistic, positive and upbeat. Have an unwavering faith in God's ability to provide for your needs. If the Universe can provide for the birds of the air, the fish of the sea, and the worms of the earth, surely it can provide for you. Remember you were created in the image and likeness of God. Therefore you have all the attributes of God available to you to use. Pray to heal your mind of a belief in fear, lack or limitation. You must keep your mind on Good things or the Goodness of the Universe on a continuous basis. Prosperity is an inner spiritual state of adequacy, abundance, fullness, love, harmony, joy, peace, and forgiveness of harm, by you against anyone.

The two emotional states that will mentally prepare you to receive prosperity are gratitude and forgiveness. Affirm daily that your every need is known by God and supplied before you ask, because God

41

loves you, and knows what you need before you ask. You were not sent to earth to fend for yourself. You are God's child, and God will take care of HIS children. You come through your parents, through the birth process. They are your human nurturer and protectors, but spiritually you belong to God.

Whatever you obtain or become in life is the result of your sustained energy and focus over a long period of time. This is why success is not a straight path. Most of us have a lot of negative mental conditioning and programming that has to be unlearned. This process of change can be likened to having a bucket of dirty water that you want to become clear water. If you replace the dirty water with a bucket full, it will get clear more quickly than if you replace the water with a spoon. However, the rate of change will be proportional to your willingness to give up your old negative thought patterns, your comfortable ways of doing things; to learn a new way of being. And be open to change and grow on a daily or hourly basis. There are many personal and professional success skills you will need to develop, before you achieve proficiency in your new endeavor. Affirm.

The Perfect Expression of Abundance

Prosperity is the nature of my perfect self. Prosperity is a state of mind. Therefore as you think, you become. Prosperity is a state of being that comes from right thinking and can only result from my recognition of the nature of my inner being. I am meant to be successful. Your freedom as a creative individualization of God enables me to achieve success in every phase of life. Prosperity, received and established in your mind, is automatically manifested in your world.

Affirm:

I have the ability to be my complete, creative, best self at all times, under any circumstance. Prosperity results from my desire and intention to express God in me.

42

There can be no limit to my prosperity, because God removes all limitation from my consciousness. As I am freed from the bondage of my fears and false beliefs, I experience true manifestation of prayer. My spiritual nature brings me real prosperity. From the center of my inner being all abundance works come forth. I identify myself with the abundance of God, and I am prosperous today.

Today I claim my affluence, abundance and prosperity. I experience fullness. I claim my good and go where I want to go and do what I want to do as long as it does not interfere with others. I affirm my prosperity. I receive and use money, knowing that it indicates spiritual prosperity. I have freedom and God is expressed fully in me when I am free. Through my word, I make known to the abundant universe what I want. Whatever I ask, I know I receive.

Our wealth and abundance flows to us in more avenues than dollars. So, it is better to focus upon all the gifts the Universe gives you: When you think about abundance or wealth, think about it as an abundance of health, a wealth of vitality or aliveness, a wealth of knowledge or clarity of thought, an abundance of enthusiasm, a wealth of supportive or caring people in your life, or your ability to give and receive love. Have you had any wonderful experiences in your life like a vacation, or has someone done something kind for you that would have cost you money if you hired someone to do it? When you think of wealth and abundance in this way it has nothing to do with dollars. Would you rather have a wealth of health or illness? Think of the many areas of your life where you see wealth and abundance and soon your wealthy beliefs will manifest as real dollars in your life

The exercises in this section will help you decide what your mission in life is. It will allow you to assess how far you have come in this process and help you determine if you have the character traits and skills needed to achieve your goal/s. It will teach you how to focus and stay focused so that you can stay motivated with your chosen vision. It will help you to make sense out of all the mumble, jumble, and chatter in your mind. You will learn the principles of success and will be able to decide by the end of the quiz if you are a candidate for success.

SELF TEST
Are You Ready For Financial Success?

1. How will your being a success change humanity.

Yes ☐ No ☐

2.Do you have a money identity.　　　　Yes ☐ No ☐

3.Do you have the self-esteem of a financial secure person.

Yes ☐ No ☐

4.What image do you have of yourself as wealthy?

Yes ☐ No ☐

5.Is your mission in life to help others become rich?

Yes ☐ No ☐

6.Do you feel a higher calling to be in business?

Yes ☐ No ☐

7.For what are you grateful about your business?

Yes ☐ No ☐

8.Do have marketing skills?　　　　Yes ☐ No ☐

9.Do you have sales skills?　　　　Yes ☐ No ☐

10. Do you have a plan to sell and promote your services or products? Yes ☐ No ☐

BIBLICAL QUOTES FOR PROSPERITY

Let the Lord be magnified, who has pleasure in the prosperity of His people. – PSALM 35:27

Thou opens Thine hand, and satisfies the desire of every living thing. – PSALM 145:16

MENTAL TREATMENT FOR UNEXPECTED MONEY

I am one with the infinite abundance of God.
   I know no separation from life.
I am a divine, perfect expression of the One God,
   who has created all of Life, continually creates Life.
This Creation is working in and through me,
   Mind acting on Mind, Life acting upon Life.
It lives through me as perfect activity.
   Right now I cease to separate myself from God.
I allow good to come into my life. I let it flow in
   easily, quickly and abundantly.
There is no great or small in the eyes of God.
   I am open to receive money, help and other resources.
I am accepting divine Good from an Infinite Source.
   I am accepting Abundance. I am expecting to prosper.
I am expecting the unexpected.
   I have no concern about paying taxes on this money.
I have no concern about paying tithes.
   I put up no barriers.
I want to believe that I can create money through fun
   as well as through hard work

45

I believe God wants me to enjoy money, life and all the splendors of life. I believe I am worthy and deserving of success, love, money and happiness

I am open and receptive to the inflow of Good in my Life.

I give thank that my prayers have been heard and answered. I praise and thank the Source of all Life.

     – REV. SHEILA ROBERTS, adapted by REV. IDA GREENE

AFFIRMATIONS FOR HEALTH AND WEALTH

I am an independent person, able to provide for myself with God's help. God is guiding me now and is with me.

I have all the money and provisions I need, available to me now.
  I will replace worry with wonder.

I will cancel and replace thoughts like "I should, could, would, have to, must, need to, "I've got to" with "I want to, I get to, I'd like to, I'd love to, and I can"

I will accept approve and appreciate myself exactly as I am no matter what the experience life is offering me

I will be independent of the good and bad opinions of others.
  I will remain centered and at peace with myself.

I will only say positive empowering things to or about others and say it in a way they understand what I say to them.

     – IDA GREENE

CHAPTER 5

HOW TO POSITION YOURSELF FOR SUCCESS

Oprah Winfrey feels we should focus on "significance" and success will follow. Ask yourself what am I doing to add significance to the world? This is what makes the great "great" Always pursue excellence and whatever you do will be significant for others. Anything is possible if you have a vision, a purpose and hold to it. The impossible becomes possible if you never quit. One of the keys to greatness is having enthusiasm or passion. If are content with mediocrity, you will see failure, not success. Sometimes the price of leadership is loneliness, therefore never be concerned about what people think about you, because only you know what you can or cannot do. Always believe in people and their potential. If people cannot help you double your income do not spend quality time with them unless you enjoy their friendship and derive pleasure from being with them.

NINE THINGS YOU CAN DO TO POSITION YOURSELF FOR SUCCESS

1. Know Your Purpose, Ask yourself what are you destined to do? What is your area of excellence, what is it that you do with little or no effort, that It is almost like breathing..

2. Define your life's work; it is when your inner direction and your work becomes play. Get feedback from others, as to what work they see you doing? Ask yourself, at what am I good?

3. To find out what is your brand, write down these words: twenty-one ways I differentiate myself from others. Then describe yourself in ten words, then five words or less.

47

4. Dedicate yourself to being a life long learner. Ask yourself who has had the greatest effect on my life and why?

5. Never let what you know impede what you do not know.

6. Show up on time.

7. Develop character and integrity and become known for these character traits.

8. Get a big vision of what you want in life; develop an inner vision of how it would look and feel; then create an outer vision of how it would look in the world.

9. Commit to excellence, don't be average. Success is a statistical event

10. Strive to have a satisfied customer, quality and quantity component to your sales. You only need one satisfied customer to get you started.

Creativity is the most important factor in life. There is an art to creating a win/win mind set. Do not think of life as a dichotomy. Things and situations can change when you learn to use the word "and" You can have this and that rather than this or that. Win/win synergy is who you know. Seek Win/Win Strategic Partnerships. In Win/Win, Networking It is who knows you, not who you know Your best network contacts will come from people who do not know you well, but heard someone mention your name or are referred by someone. Entrepreneurs network from communications or notions. The entrepreneur is the best network to have. You will need a data base of contacts with constant updates. You will need structural co-operations like Joint Venture or Co-Op Ventures. Align yourself with people who have a database of names not like yours or a business different from yours and offer to create a joint venture with them.

You want to keep yourself in the mind of your customer at all times. You want people to think of you first before they think of anyone else. Pay close attention to determine what your client or customer needs. Ask yourself, what am I doing to bring comprehensive services to my customers? How am I keeping my self updated?

Ask yourself, if I removed any restraints on my life where would I be? Don't let you, anyone or anything hold you back. Remove all mental restraints on what you can or cannot do today.

The above article was contributed by F.J. Spencer. He can be reached by email at fj.spencer@imsw.com

QUICK TIPS for use of the phone

You all know that a crisp, professional voice mail greeting is essential for your business. Here are some helpful details that you may have overlooked:

- Use a clear, strong voice. Don't make your caller work to understand you.

- If your greeting is long and informative, give instructions to bypass the greeting up front.

- Customize your greeting, as in:
  "Today is Tuesday, September 30. I will be out of the office and unable to retrieve messages until after 2 PM."

If you roll over your office calls to your home or cell phone, make sure you have a clear professional voice mail greeting on them as well. Preferably it is exactly the same as your office voice mail greeting to have consistency for your caller.

Know when not to answer your phone. If you are at a train station with a train arriving or departing, don't answer your cell. Let your voice mail take over. If you are at home and your two-year-old is throwing a tantrum? Don't use the phone. Return the call when you can focus on the business to be discussed, without unbusinesslike distractions. Use your email auto-responder when you know you won't be able to answer your email within a 24-hour period.

Be professional, Professionals make it easy and pleasant to do business with them. People want to do business with the person who is easy to work with.

SELF TEST – BUSINESS SUCCESS INVENTORY

1. I know what I want out of life?   Yes ☐ No ☐
2. I have chosen a business that blends with my personality, abilities and interests?   Yes ☐ No ☐
3. I know my business strengths and weaknesses. I have taken measures to utilize the services and skills of others who balance my weaknesses.   Yes ☐ No ☐
4. I have accepted that I will need the services of competent professionals for my business growth, and I am willing to pay for these services.   Yes ☐ No ☐
5. I have financial and quantitative goals for myself and my business?   Yes ☐ No ☐
6. Do you have an action plan to accomplish these goals and are they tied to a time frame?   Yes ☐ No ☐
7. Are you a self-disciplined person?   Yes ☐ No ☐
8. Are you willing to work long hours or sacrifice?   Yes ☐ No ☐
9. Do you have expertise in your chosen field?   Yes ☐ No ☐
10. Do you enjoy the work you do?   Yes ☐ No ☐

11. Would you do what you are doing if you received no income?

Yes ☐ No ☐

12. Is this career choice your mission in life?   Yes ☐ No ☐

There are no right or wrong answers to this quiz. Your chance of business success increases if you can answer yes to all questions. Retake, this quiz once a month to see how you have progressed.

Salesmanship – All successful entrepreneurs need a course in salesmanship. All of life is about selling. You will need to sell someone on the idea, you are the best person for the job, and that they need to hire you. You may need to sell the people working under you or over you on a new idea you would like to put into effect. You may need to sell your boss on the idea that you deserve a promotion or a salary increase. Do take a class in selling. If nothing else you will learn how to sell you on you. You are a product, and you are a commodity. You have skills and talents. You have value. Will you be undersold? Who will decide how much you are worth?

To move to the top of the success ladder you will need to sell your services and talents and no one knows how valuable you are, but you. Are you worth the effort and time someone would need to pay if they hired you? If you cannot resoundingly say yes to these questions, begin to work on your self-esteem; seek the assistance of professionals who can help you. Be willing to pay to become a better product (person). Be realistic and honest with yourself. Seek ways to improve yourself. You are a commodity. Are you a Volkswagen or Mercedes Benz? It's all a state of mind. The mind is the creative cause of all that transpires in a person's life. Our personal conditions are the results of our actions and our actions are the results of the thoughts and ideas we think.

IT'S ALL IN THE STATE OF MIND

If You Think You Are Beaten, You Are,
If You Think You Dare Not, You Don't
If You Like To Win, But You Think You Can't
It Is Almost Certain You Won't.
If You Think You'll Lose, You're Lost,
For Out In The World We Find
Success Begins With A Fellow's Will
It's All In The State Of Mind.
If You Think You Are Outclassed, You Are,
You've Got To Be Sure Of Yourself Before
You Can Ever Win A Prize.
Life's Battles Don't Always Go
To The Stronger Or Faster Man,
But Soon Or Late The Person Who Wins
Is The Person Who Thinks They Can.

— ANON

A Drive to Action – This is where you pull together all of the above traits and characteristics into concrete, realistic, effective action. Whereby you take advantage of the opportunities afforded you and transcends the obstacles before you.

Life in its great and wonderful abundance is pouring itself out to us as unexpected good, in the form of unexpected money.
Affirm this by stating out loud, "I now claim for myself, unexpected money on a daily basis:"

AFFIRM
Today there is nothing I can do, say, think, or become that establishes my worth, my self-worth comes from God.

52 Tips To Sell Your Services Profitably

Tip #1

Get focused and make sure **Everything** you do reflects that focus.

Tip #2

Learn the **buzzwords** that your target market responds to, and use them in your materials

Tip #3

Consider exhibiting at trade shows. It takes 62% less effort to close a sale from a lead generated at a trade show than one generated in the field.

Tip #4

Find a way for your clients to sample your services. Sample selling is the BEST selling technique in the world!

Tip #5

Use voice mail to leave a sales message. 15 seconds of promotional material, carefully scripted, can get you a "warm" callback.

Tip #6

Ask the client **"What else can I do for you?"**. The concept is a basic sales technique and increases business by over 10%!

Tip #7

Add in something **Extra for Free**. It doesn't have to be expensive and it shows the client that you care.

Tip #8

Use postcards to contact clients. They're full color, cost less than 50 cents total, and get read, even if they get tossed out!

Tip #9

Tease clients with a giveaway. For example, send them ? the article and require that they contact you to get the other half.

Tip #10

Tape an interesting story about your services and air it on local television stations. Cable stations are required to air your material for **FREE!**

Tip #11

Remember to use **magic words** in your advertising message like **New, Now, At Last, Amazing, Fast, Easy, Introducing, Unique, Free, Breakthrough, Sale, or Special.**

Tip #12

Make yourself known with silly publicity. Represent yourself as the **"Newly Discovered Prince of [your service] and will be holding audience with selected clients who make an appointment.".** Get an artist to graphically represent you with a crown and robe to make it look real.

Tip #13

Use classic headlines in your material-they work. For great basic guidelines check out www.marketingtoday.com/marcom/writeads.htm

Tip #14

Tie the advertising of your services to the needs of your clients. Write articles that show how your services benefit their industries and submit them to the industry trade journals for publication.

Tip #15

Write articles for your client's publications. Include the firm's decision makers in your articles and they'll become your champion in the organization and remember you rather than your competition.

Tip #16
Send thank you notes, letters, and gifts to **Past** clients. It'll remind them that you're still around and they appreciate them.

Tip #17
Guarantee your work, unconditionally, and in writing. It implies zero risk and makes the buying decision easier for the client.

Tip #18
If you can't be the prime contractor, try to be the sub contractor. Contact the winner of the job and see if you can do part of the work.

Tip #19
Donate some services in your industry where they will be **seen and appreciated**. It's tax deductible and good PR.

Tip #20
Ask for referrals – every time. If you've done a good job, you'll get plenty. If you've forgotten, use this opportunity as an excuse to call on past clients.

Tip #21
Give people something of value for referrals – not just a thank you!

Tip #22
Find a mutually beneficial way to partner with another service provider. You can share articles, leads, and marketing efforts.

Tip #23
Look at the services you provide and look for everyday changes that would create a need for that service. Voila! Target market revealed!

Tip #24

Ask for feedback! If your clients think you're truly concerned about their needs, they'll respond and you'll get more business because you're straightforward.

Tip #25

Survey your clients by telephone. People are busy and if they can answer a few short questions over the phone rather than filling out a survey form, they're more likely to do it. Be sure to thank them for their time with a gift.

Tip #26

Offer to do a FREE needs analysis. You'll learn a lot about clients' needs and how to position yourself better in the future.

Tip #27

Get published and you'll become and instant authority in your field! The public bestows people who are published authors with credibility.

Tip #28

Record an audiotape session of questions and answers that pertain to your field of expertise. Audiotapes make great sales samples and can be sold if packaged.

Tip #29

Get yourself booked on radio talk shows. You'll get to be the expert who reveals important facts and details questions in your field of expertise and have lots of people find out who you are.

Tip #30

The web is a big library, so write an electronic book with lots of valuable information that your clients can use. Tell them how to find it with conventional advertising. Get everything you need to create a web site for FREE at www.RoundsMiller.com/update.htm

Tip #31

Audiotape interviews with several clients who are experts in your field. Send the tapes to prospective clients so that they know that you're an expert too.

Tip #32

Do some clever advertising that features you in a memorable manner like: *"You do not know me – I do Not look familiar to you"*. *Federal Witness Protection Program.*

Tip #33

Give out FREE coupons for some of your service time on your web site--but require that they answer a few questions to receive the coupons.

Tip #34

To get people to read your entire web site, mail prospective clients a quiz with a nice prize for all the correct answers (like a box of chocolates). Let them know that the answers are on the web site.

Tip #35

Remember the two rules for successfully selling services: #1 Follow the money. #2 see Rule #1. If there's no money there, don't waste your time.

Tip #36

Create a two-sided, 8.5 x 11 inch **"Tips Card"** with information that is important to the industry you service. Include your contact information and have the card laminated.

Tip #37

Swap your services for advertising in a client's publication. It'll give you an implied endorsement by the organization and keep your name in front of your target industry.

Tip #38

Remember the client's important dates like birthdays, holidays and anniversaries. Use <u>www.bluemountain.com</u> to send FREE greetings.

Tip #39

Become the industry GURU by setting up an electronic advisory board on the web. Ask your clients to refer their inquiries and problems to "The Pro" and tell them that you'll respond via e-mail for FREE!

Tip #40

Speak once or write an article for FREE for a client or prospective client if they'll give you their mailing list or if they'll give you a FREE ad in their organization's publication.

Tip #41

Create an E-Book with lots of tips, tricks, and information that your clients can use using *Adobe Acrobat*®. Offer it free from your web site, but only after they fill in a questionnaire.

Tip #42

Keep accurate records and follow up on a regular basis with your clients. Contact management software like ACT® will help you.

Tip #43

Give FREE educational seminar with LOTS of valuable information. Use the seminar to generate leads for a paid program or to sell them your services directly.

Tip #44
Get business cards with your picture on them especially, if you're the one performing the services.

Tip #45
Write and talk about your accomplishments, then mail the material to your clients with reproduction rights. Remember: *"It ain't braggin' if you've done it!"*

Tip #46
Write, mail and e-mail press releases about your successes to the client's publications, the industry trade journals and the public newspapers. They're usually starved for human-interest stories about successes.

Tip #47
Donate public education seminars about your field of expertise to the local library in return for notoriety.

Tip #48
Send thank you letters when you lose a job. The client will have other needs and if you're right there with them through the good and the bad times, they'll remember you.

Tip #49
Survey your client base to see what they want. Submit the results in article form to an industry trade journal and send everybody who participate a thank you letter and a copy of the article.

Tip #50
Never make excuses for problems. Instead, apologize and rectify them immediately, even if it costs you. Most "customer service" is lip service these days and if you really make good on your commitments, you'll be remembered, hired, and referred.

Tip #51

Ask your existing clients what areas they think you should expand into. After they tell, you, see if you can't book some business with them in the areas that they just defined.

Tip #52

Write a Tips booklet like this one for your area of expertise. You can sell it or give it to your clients as a way of saying thank you for their patronage.

The above article was contributed by F.J. Spencer. He can be reached by email at fj.spencer@imsw.com

Chapter 6

How to Be a Marketing Guru

Nothing happens in business until a transaction occurs and a sale is made. Marketing is everything that takes place leading up to the sale. Marketing is the awareness and insight you get from listening to the client about the goals or objectives they want to achieve, their needs, life style and unique positioning of them or their product.

Your ability to market yourself and your business is the key to your success or failure in business. Everything revolves around selling in some form. However, marketing is the "life line" of your business, it is critical that you know the difference between marketing and sale. Marketing should be an on going activity for your business over time. Marketing includes the following:

1. Branding, a brand name, logo and a business tag line that lets others know what you do
2. Business Cards
3. Advertisement
4. Direct mail
5. Speaking
6. Seminars /workshop
7. Direct mail
8. Books, E-books.

Business Building Secrets

1. Marketing is the number one most important thing you will do to build your business. What is your strategic marketing plan? Do you have one? Is it well thought out? Does it include multiple

marketing channels? Financially successful companies put 50-65% of their resources into marketing.

2. Marketing is your best business leverage tool; because for every dollar, you spend on marketing you can get a return revenue of another dollar or thousands of dollars. The amount of return for every dollar you invest in marketing depends on how good your marketing programs are and how many channels you have.

3. Referral Marketing is the cheapest, fastest and best form of marketing. Why? Because it gives you your best marketing leverage. You can spend very little on encouraging and causing referrals and you can get many new clients in return.

4. Have a formal Referral Reward system. Don't just ask for referrals; encourage them with a formal incentive system called your Referral Reward. Your current customer/client base, including friends, associates and family should be rewarded for referring you to others. It just guarantees more and more referrals. Get creative. Referral Rewards don't need to be money. You can joint venture with another company to supply the reward in exchange for exposure and promotion.

5. Have a Risk Reversal policy. This means have a money back guarantee. People will feel more trusting and it encourage those prospects who are already very interested to make the final purchase decision.

6. Have a quality, professional website that presents you, your services or products to your market. Having a website is quickly becoming a must-have marketing medium. You can no longer treat it like a glorified brochure or business card. You must make it your business portal, a way to communicate, a way to do business.

7. Get marketing and business skills. You won't be very successful in business today without them. There is just too much competition in the marketplace. With so much information available to obtain these skills, you also have no excuse for not being wildly successful. Ask an experienced Business Coach like myself or someone you have researched to mentor or coach you. Buy a book on marketing

Measure everything you do for marketing your business. This is the only way you will know whether you are reaching your goals and whether your marketing ideas and tactics are working as well as you want them to work. Create a chart and measurement criteria. Then you can know exactly what is producing the most leads and sales . Create a system that works for you and use it over and over to improve the system.

YOU AND SALES
Sales includes the following:
1. Personal Self-Esteem
2. Self-Image
3. Business Self-Image
4. Success Identity
5. Self-Confidence
6. Management of the following Fears
   a. Fear of Failure
   b. Fear of Success
   c. Fear of Criticism
   d. Fear of Rejection
   e. Fear of Unworthiness/Undeserving
   f. Fear of Poverty
   g. Fear of Money

MASTERING THE ART OF CLOSING A SALE
by Diane Dermer

Whether you are learning how to Close for the first time, or are polishing up your technique, here are some helpful words of advice found in the Dynamics of Creative Selling program.

Genuine excitement, deep personal satisfaction and supreme confidence are your rewards for becoming a master of the art of closing sales. You can never call yourself a real salesperson unless you can close a sale. You may be a fine conversationalist, and you may be entertaining and well-liked, but these qualities alone are not enough to qualify you as a master salesperson. You must develop the ability to close sales, to reach your goal of becoming a top professional and to attain the income, prestige and sense of well-being that you deserve. There are no deep, dark secrets of closing

The foundations of a Close

Closing is a skill that can be learned through study and practice. There are two basic principles that form the foundation of an effective close:

1　The sale cannot be closed until the prospect is ready to buy. We have to take our prospects through the sales process. We have to answer questions.

2.　The art of closing is not getting the prospect to make decisions. It is the art of making decisions with which the prospect will agree. As the seller, you make the decision that the prospect is going to buy. The close is a natural and logical result of an effective sales presentation.

The process of closing a sale actually begins when you get your prospect. It is much easier to close a Class A prospect than any other prospect. The more information you have on the prospect and his or her market, the more prepared you will be for the close. You can find out quite a bit of information about your prospect while you're setting the appointment on the telephone. This information will be very helpful in your close.

What Is a Sales Close?

It's important to know exactly what a close is. A close is asking for information on the credit application or asking for money five times. "Which would be better for you, the total investment or the time investment?" The question is designed to ask how they will pay, not if they will buy.

Qualities of a Good Closing Statement

A good closer has several qualities:

1. **A closer knows the numbers.** A good closer knows the value of their close. If you sell one out of three closes, every close is worth $200. A good closer knows their numbers will work for them.

2. **A closer is a "product of the product."** As a product of the product, you have controlled attention and concentrated energy. You know how the prospect will benefit because you have already benefited from the program.

3. **A good closer is a good prospector and qualifier**. A good prospector/qualifier doesn't have to ask, "Why am I here talking to this person?"

4. **A good closer is a decision-maker.** You make the decision that the prospect is going to buy.

5. **A good closer understands how people think and understands the psychology of selling.** Lesson Nine, "Courage to Close" in the Dynamics of Creative Selling has great information on developing these attitudes.

6. **A good closer is prepared to close.** You have the order pad, the application, the security agreement, and something to write with. It's important to be both physically and mentally prepared. Visualize yourself going through the close with the prospect.

7. **A good closer knows their purpose for being there**. The purpose is to make a sale. Remember why you are there.

An Inventory to Assess Your Sales Ability

1. **It Does Not**
   a. Measure intelligence
   b. Measure mental health
   c. Give right or wrongs

2. **What It Does:**
   a. Increases understanding of your style and the strengths of others
   b. Provides guidelines for increasing your effectiveness

3. **It Assumes:**
   a. All people have styles of behavior and personality
   b. All styles have strengths
   c. Weaknesses are often strengths taken to excess or overused
   d. Behavioral Styles may change under stress
   e. We need all types
   f. Behavioral Styles impact group efficiency, effectiveness, innovation and creativity

4. **The Three Behavioral Styles Are:**
   a. Altruistic – Nurturing
   b. Analytic-Autonomizing behavior
   c. Assertive – Directive

Nurturing → Altruistic Type

Altruistic and **Nurturing** types *feel best about what they are doing,* when they are being helpful to others who can genuinely benefit from their help.

These folks *feel most rewarded by others* when they are treated as a warm and friendly person who wants to be of help and who is deserving of thanks and appreciation for giving help. These people feel *distant from and somewhat contemptuous of* people who constantly compete with and try to take advantage of others or who are cold and unresponsive to gestures of friendliness.

66

Nurturing and Altruistic People:

Strengths →	Weaknesses
Trusting	Gullible
Idealistic	Wishful
Modest	Self-Effacing
Caring	Smothering
Accepting	Passive
Optimistic	Impractical
Helpful	Self-Denying
Devoted	Self-Sacrificing
Supportive	Submissive

Assertive/Directing Type

Strengths →	Weaknesses
Self-Confident	Arrogant
Enterprising	Opportunistic
Ambitious	Ruthless
Organizer	Controlling
Persuasive	Pressuring
Forceful	Dictatorial
Quick to Act	Rash
Competitive	Combative
Risk-taker	Gambler

Adapted from the Strength Deployment Inventory

POSITIVE THOUGHTS

God provides the victuals, but He does not cook the meal.
– ANONYMOUS

The principal maker of genius is not perfection but originality, the opening of new frontiers. – ARTHUR KOESTLER

DAILY PROSPERITY MESSAGES

I am one with the infinite Supply of the Universe. It knows me, claims me, and rushes to me.

I accept this Supply for myself and for everyone..

Prosperity is the law of my life. This law is continuously operative in my affairs.

I now open my mind, body, purse, business, and all else in order that this prosperity may flow through me in abundant measure.

I am confident that I shall have plenty to meet every need when it is due.

My income is in the keeping of infinite wisdom. My affairs are guided by Divine Intelligence.

All that the Father hath is mine now. Today I claim my good and today it is mine.

Prosperity flows through me in an uninterrupted stream, eliminating everything unlike itself. There is nothing in me that can obstruct, congest, or retard my supply in any way.

My Supply is wherever I am. It comes to me from everywhere.

I accept my abundance, bounty, and opulence today. I know that it is externalizing itself in my life and affairs.

I am not concerned about the limitations and fears of yesterday. I know that right now everything is made rich.

I deny that I am broke, despondent, poor, crushed, defeated, or dependent.

New opportunities are now opening for me.

Wherever I go, I meet prosperous people and prosperous conditions.

I let blessings, money, and possessions flow to me from every direction.

I believe the law of Prosperity operating through me will bless and
   enrich everyone I meet.
I do not identify with lack, but practice the Presence of God.
         – REVEREND, DR. DELIA SELLERS

Here are some Chants (words you can say) to help condition your
mind to receive money

I let go all poverty thoughts or thoughts of lack and limitation.

*Money comes to me through many sources, in increasing amounts on
   a continuous basis.*

I think and feel like the wealthy

I use my money wisely and spend frugally like the wealthy

I save money like the wealthy

I invest 10% of my income like the wealthy

I pay my bills cheerfully and on time, therefore my credit is good.

Chapter 7

How to Survive in the Business World

We create our world through our thoughts about life in general and ourselves in particular. If you are clear in your thinking and affirmative in your mind, you will find self fulfillment because you will attract positive conditions, and positive constructive people, like yourself. Though we are not able to control the circumstances of our life; we are able to control our response to people, situations, circumstances and events through our beliefs. Anything you believe with an air of positive expectancy will happen. Therefore, if you desire success, wealth, abundance and riches believe you will achieve it. Believe this with deep feeling and you will experience and manifest it.

To have success or be successful, you must first create a success consciousness or mind set. Everything is created first from a thought pattern. All ideas, purpose, plans, or desires are created in your thoughts first before they become a reality. Through the law of attraction, we can change any undesirable conditions. It requires the ability to control your thoughts to correspond to the desired conditions and objectives you have set in your mind. The mind can only hold one thought at a time: Lack, prosperity, scarcity or abundance, poverty or wealth, success or failure. You can choose to focus on prosperity, abundance, wealth, or success.

You must be willing to take risks, to go forth on your faith of seeing a perfect outcome, even though it may not be visible. One way to do this is to raise your body's energy vibration until you are able to manifest what you desire.

Twelve Commitments That Will Exponentially Raise Your Manifesting Vibration. (Jafree Ozwald)

1. I always decide to accept, approve, love, and appreciate myself exactly as I am no matter what the situation or experience I am going through.

2. I always replace heavy and weak thoughts with light and powerful thoughts. For example, "I need to, I have to, I've got to, I should, I could, and I would", are replaced with, "I'd love to, I want to, I get to, I can, I will, and I am."

3. I remain centered and at peace with myself whenever others are not.

4. I explore each experience in life (especially those that trouble me) with a gentle compassionate energy, and childlike curiosity.

5. I easily create life-long fulfilling relationships, allowing my heart and mind to be open to fully accepting and even loving every person and situation that comes my way.

6. I always replace worry with wonder.

7. I have healthy boundaries with respect to the demands of others and can easily say NO to someone who may try to make me feel victimized, taken advantage of or dis-empowered in any way.

8. I am independent of the good and bad opinions of other people.

9. I speak ONLY positive empowering statements about others and myself.

10. I exercise, meditate, eat healthy, and get enough sleep at least six days per week.

11. I Only do inspired actions in my life.

12. I am 100% committed to practicing these commitments no matter what happens for the next 90 days.

"There are basically two movements of consciousness:
Love and Fear. Love is allowing what is and fear is resisting it."
– NIRMALA

Your passion is anything that brings you joy and satisfaction, something you do easily and effortlessly like breathing. It makes you wonder why you are getting paid because you would do it without pay.

TO DISCOVER YOUR PASSION,
Ask Yourself These Questions

1. **What things in life gives me the greatest pleasure. Write them now**
   a. Personal

   b. Professional

   c. Social

   d. Spiritual

2. What things do others praise or compliment me on? Am I doing this type of work?

3. What things or activities would I do if I were not paid?

4. What is it that I do easily without effort and never tire?

5. What are some ways I can turn my passion into a profit-making business?

To Assess Your Strengths and Talents

1. Name characteristics or traits you have that set you apart from others.

2. To find your weaknesses:
   List areas of your personality you want to improve.

3. To Enhance Your Self-Image, ask yourself, how do I see my self in relation to other persons with similar skills?

   a. Create an image of what you would like to do, or become. Take five minutes each day and reflect on the new person you will be.

b.   Create a picture collage from magazines of people who possess the skills you want and have the amount of money you desire. Put a picture of yourself in the center.
Put this poster above your bed so you can see it when you go to bed at night and when you awake in the morning

A SIMPLIFIED BUSINESS PLAN

There are at least three basic premises about a business plan. You can use it monthly to see how well you have achieved your goals. You can easily explain it to someone who is interested in your success, e.g. your significant other, spouse, or your coach.

First – Write a brief outline of what you want to have, be or do.
Second – Draft a plan that is simple, uncomplicated and meaningful.
Third – Use this as a plan for what you want to do with your business. The simple business plan is *seven* pages long, this is the order of completing the pages:

Page 2 – Write who you are and what you do. What is your business and what benefits the purchasers of your services (products) get when they buy your services or (products)?

Page 3 – Who or what specifically is your market?

Page 4 – How are you going to reach the buyer of your services or products?

Page 5 – What is your projection of income, expense and profit on a monthly basis for the year.

Page 6 – What is your projection of the best possible results you could obtain for the year and projection of minimum acceptable results you will accept.

Page 7 – This is a Five Year projection. Write a description of where you are now and what you want to have achieved in five years with your business.

Now comes **Page 1** – This is a one-page summary of your business plan. Keep it to one page. Include your mission statement, and vision for your business. Keep the format clear, concise and have fun doing it.
— SANDRA SCHRIFT (*modified by Ida Greene*)

How To Get What You Want In Life
You Can Have Anything You Want
If You Want It Badly Enough.
You Can Be Anything You Want To Be,
Have, Anything You Set Out To Accomplish
If You Will Hold To That Desire
With Singleness of Purpose.
— ROBERT COLLIER

I Accept my Self, Health, and Wealth

It is right, and just for me to have my needs met.
It is right and just for me to ask for and receive what I want.
I am accepting of others showing appreciation and love to me.
I am deserving of love, affection, good treatment, and respect. I am
*   created in the image and likeness of God, it feels good.*
I am created in the image of God, who is perfection of body, mind,
*   and soul.*
God cares for me and provides for all my needs.
I do not need to ask, my loving God already knows what I need.
I am proud to have a rich, royal, wise and spiritual lineage.
All of my needs are abundantly supplied. I now cease all worry and
*   concern so that God can work through me.*

75

I know I am loved beyond measure; God wants the best for me.
I give up all struggle as, I allow God to point the way.
I am patient with myself, and God as I evolve to my higher self.
I am a better person each day. I am worthy to be God's child. I accept
  all of God's creation, starting with myself.
                        – IDA GREENE

HOW TO SEE YOUR CURRENT BUSINESS CLEARLY
Write the answers to these questions on a sheet of paper

What goals or outcomes are you ready to achieve?

What might stop you in achieving your goals?

What specifically is great about your business?

What are you fed up with?

What is your reason for being in business?

What is the biggest challenge facing you in your business?

What do you want to get out of your business?

What is your job description?

What value do you provide your customers/clients?

What can your clients/customers expect from you?

What are the standards you live by in your business?

What are your current assets, liabilities, income, expenses and net worth?

How are you positioning your business in the marketplace?

In an ideal month what would your business revenues be?

In an ideal month what would be your personal income?

How much time do you want off and when?

How can you grow your business to where the potential is unlimited?
– KEN FOSTER

Chapter 8

How to Break Through the Blocks to Your Success

The Essential Step to Get Anything You Want.

There are a lot of reasons why people get frustrated or struggle in life. One of the most common reason is that some people are lazy and refuse to get started. Some people have big dreams but refuse to take the first steps to make them come true. Thinking about something will not cause it to happen. The biggest obstacle is fear of the unknown. Success is always an unknown. It is uncharted territory, we are always creating something new each minute of the day. Success can not be predicted, confined or defined. It is you and your life in continuous progress. As long as you are breathing and doing you are creating something. You are a work of art in progress.

A word or thought over a period of time can create a debilitating and life threatening condition in your body. Shakespeare said, "There is nothing good or bad, but thinking makes it so." The only meaning any event has in our lives is the interpretation we give it. It does not matter whether it is real or imagined. If we experience the events and situations as negative, and continually view them as threatening, conflicting, or fearful, we can expect to see permanent debilitating, destructive physiological changes in our body.

Often, when we are confronted with a stressful situation, our ability to problem solve is ineffective, due to prior learned ways of perceiving and reacting to stressors. You may have learned or developed a distorted mental framework, whereby you fail to see the obvious due to your automatic thoughts or behaviors. The painful experiences

78

we encounter in life are growth producing, because they make us stretch beyond our comfort zone. Discomfort is a necessary part of "the good life" you seek- Pray for persistence, determination, emotional stamina, patience to endure the dark moments in your life, and the faith to wait on God's divine timing, divine illumination to know when to act, when to be still, and when to go within for divine guidance. Say to yourself, I am healed of all negative stress about this matter. Then Let It Go.

Self-management is a do-it-yourself job. We cannot gain control of our outer world until we master our inner world. Our inner world is often torn with strife, dissension, and unrest. I call this inner turmoil "the demon within us," for it tends to surface at the most inappropriate and inconvenient times. This demon within may take the form of stress, anxiety, fear, confusion, frustration, impatience, worry, anticipation, power, control, resentment, jealousy, envy, greed, or hatred. The demon, fear, seems to be ingrained within our collective unconscious mind (the collective race mind of us.)

Within our inner world, the emotion of fear, is the most difficult to eradicate or modify. It can be destructive to our body, mind, and soul, if not managed properly. There is good in fear. It alerts us to impending dangerous situations. However, when fear is allowed to go beyond its limited useful boundaries, it becomes all-pervasive, all-consuming, and destructive. Fear must be managed at all times to best serve us. Fear impedes the development of trust and faith; which are essential character traits for the evolvement of our individual, emotional, and spiritual growth. Energy always precedes manifestation. Therefore, our greatest intention is always acted upon. Our intention, or intent, creates an anticipatory set of behaviors based on prior learned behavioral patterns. They allow us the opportunity to move forward with our plans, to create and manifest what we desire. If your fear level is low to moderate, you can create what you desire.

When your fear level is high, you become immobilized with apprehension and anxiety, due to prior misconceived data, or false imaginings of your mind. Fear is a behavioral response in the body brought about by a physiologically real or imagined threat to the maintenance and status quo of our physiological, emotional, and mental systems.

Medical science now says that every single emotion we feel has an impact on some part of our body. Fear produces muscular tension, an over abundance of hydrochloric acid in the stomach, constriction of arteries, hypertension, muscular aches, over-tiredness, and a seemingly unending list of ailments. Emotionally, fear drives people away from us, makes us "needy," desperate, and lonely. Making us angry, "uptight," and insecure.

What is fear? How do we get it? Where does it come from? Does everyone experience fear? Fear is an irrational belief about a thing, idea, or event that seems real to the observer, even in the face of reality, which indicates that there is no logical observable basis for the fear. At the root of all fear is a thought form that was perceived in error, which on a previous occasion was associated with an activity that had no prior frame of reference to draw upon. The outcome was uncertain, thereby creating a situation of panic because the subconscious mind did not know how to handle the situation. The subconscious mind is the controller and manipulator of events in our inner and outer world.

When the subconscious mind finds itself in unfamiliar terrain, it will attempt to escape from the situation to spare us embarrassment, or avoid having to figure out the matter. *The subconscious mind is not a risk taker.* It functions mainly as a computer to store and catalog the events and situations in our life. It has a corresponding behavioral template (back up system) for every activity we have encountered in the past. It works on an automatic relay of a behavior response system. Whenever the conscious mind is given a challenge or presented with a situation, our subconscious mind has in its memory bank all of the behavioral reactions that occurred in the past, and it immediately relays them through a nerve impulse, and the behavior is manifested. We may experience, for example, tightness in the shoulders, constriction in the stomach, shaky knees, sweaty palms, or whatever bodily response our body has exhibited in the past. When we are faced with a stressor, we may notice and experience one or a combination of the above physiological responses or we may experience an entirely different reaction.

If we are in touch with our emotions, and desire to change the way we react to the people, situations, and events in our lives, we can choose to respond differently and create a new neuronal pathway for a new behavioral response. However, if we exhibit a new behavioral response to an old behavioral pattern it means that there is and has been a conscious effort on our part to input new data into the memory bank of our mind and to delete or neutralize the prior mental neuronal input. In order for us to experience a change in behavior; we must consciously input new behavioral data into our memory bank.

Thoughts are things and our state of consciousness produces its corresponding behavior. What we see in the outer world is a mirror of our inner thought patterns. All there is in the universe is energy. Fear begins as an idea or thought seed in our consciousness. Just as a seed, if nourished with energy, right nutrients and soil grows, to sprout into a plant or flower; so it is with a fear thought.

When a fear thought seedling is planted in the subconscious mind and given energy (ideal nutrient for growth and survival), it grows to become large and powerful. Each time we act out a fear response, and respond in a fearful manner, we add more energy to the original idea/fear pattern. And the more energy a fear thought gets, the larger it becomes.

Eventually, the constant repetition of fear reinforcements causes the fear thought form to enlarge until it consumes and controls our behavioral responses. Then it is called free floating anxiety. In this form, the person does not have to think fearful thoughts anymore. The fear stimulus has now become cued to many random behavioral responses, and any stimulus that closely resembles the original fear thought form will elicit the fear response in the body.

To eradicate fear from your conscious mind, you must not entertain fear thoughts through worry or doubt. Fear thoughts are very powerful. You only need to listen to another person express doubt or fear in your presence to activate your old programmed mental fear tapes previously recorded in your mind. When this happens, the experience becomes alive and real to you, as if it was occurring in the present moment. We are all energy fields, states of consciousness; therefore, if we listen to another person express fear and we are sympathetic to their cause, it can affect us. The vibrations of their energy field can spillover into yours and make yours a part of their emotional field.

You must always stand guard at the door of your consciousness (mind), so that you allow only what is good and beneficial to enter your light. Remember, we all have our individual energy fields (states of consciousness); however, there is the collective mind consciousness where all energy thoughts come together. Jung referred to this as the collective unconscious or race thought. These are the beliefs held by the majority of people. An example of this is, most Americans believe in democracy.

If your energy field has a weak link, it becomes a part of whatever energy field is present. If your thought form does not have a strong electromagnetic charge (strong belief), which is greater than the opposing thought's electromagnetic field, it will not repel the energy charge of the opposing thought.

You can choose the way you look at and experience life. If things are not to your liking, you can rearrange your circumstances and implement changes into your life, that are more to your liking, or in harmony with your life style. You can see a bucket half empty or you can see it half full. Likewise, you can view the loss of a job as an opportunity to start a new career, or you can see it as the end of the road.

Our ability to cope with the stressors of life is directly proportional to the words we say to ourselves about the events that occur to us. For example, If you were laid off or terminated from work, you could say something like this to yourself; "I can develop a plan to deal with this situation." Or if you are a spiritual person, you might say, "God has a better plan for my life and it is being revealed to me now.

Here are some things you can do to cope more effectively with stress or stressful situations: Use a problem solving approach. To do this, you must first define the problem. Why not try this now? Get a blank sheet of paper.

First, write out the problem/s you are now experiencing, in as much detail as possible.

Second, analyze the problem. Break it down into smaller parts so that you can identify the problem.

Third, brainstorm by listing or writing down on a piece of paper all the possible solutions to the problem.
Fourth, tackle the problem as if you had a high expectation of a successful outcome.

Fifth, look at and accept all adequate or reasonable solutions. The solution does not need to be perfect or be the best one. Now evaluate each solution against a list of criteria that states the conditions you desire, and then select the best one.

Sixth, persist until you find a solution. You may want or need to adopt a new approach, add new resources, change your strategy or schedule. Lastly, begin to implement the program. Try out some things to see how they work. If things do not work as you would like, go back through this process again.

One of Newton's laws says that for every action there is an equal and opposite reaction. Tony Robbins is famous for his observation that high achievers take massive action. They observe their results, adjust accordingly, and take more action. There is tremendous power in persistent, determined action. There is a famous phrase in the Bible that says the "truth shall set you free" and a key truth is that to achieve any goal, no matter what it is, some action, effort, work, activity, physical exertion is required and the activity must come "First". To achieve your goals, action is required. Often the required action is simple, easy and obvious.

Over my years as a coach, I've had conversations with people who want to reach ordinary sort of goals that a lot of other people have achieved. They want to save for retirement, start a business, travel the world, or do something that seemed difficult to them, but has been achieved by a lot of other people. The problem is they "could not find a way" to take the first steps to achieve their success. They hesitated to get started, "could not" find a way to save money, nor develop the first draft of a business plan. For them their pain and frustrations were real, however their fear prevented them from achieving success, their fear was in their mind.

Often, the steps are simple, easy and obvious. The key is to get started, take a small action, observe your results, adjust accordingly, and then take more action. Most of the actions people take when they set out to achieve a goal are "Wrong". We learn by trial and error. When we try anything for the first time, we are bound to make mistakes, but mistakes are not a sign of failure. They are the best decision or smartest action we could think of at the time, they may not give us the results we desire, so we learn and try again.

Did you fall down when you first tried to walk? Was your first attempt at dating clumsy or embarrassing? Were your first attempts to use a computer frustrating? There is no failure or shame in trying. We try, we learn, and we try again. The key to getting anything you want in life is to take action. Take the smartest, best action you can think of and see what happens. It is best if you can, hire a mentor or coach to help you. but take some action. Observe your results, adjust accordingly, and keep on keeping on.

FAMOUS QUOTES
In any moment of decision, the best thing you can do is the right thing. The worst thing you can do is nothing.
– THEODORE ROOSEVELT

Affirmations
Stay in the present. Avoid statements like, "I will" or "I hope to." Instead, say, "I am."

Work on only a few affirmations at a time.

To help you get started, I have made a long list of affirmations. After you get used to them, you may want to substitute others that more closely apply to your individual situation. Remember each time to fill in your own name after the "I".

Here are some suggested affirmations that you can begin working with to break through your Fears of Success:

85

To Change Your Fear of Success, Affirm:
1. I am seeing a positive image of myself.

2. I am seeing myself with an abundance of love.

3. I am seeing myself with an abundance of prosperity.

4. I am seeing myself successful

5. I am seeing myself happy and healthy.

6. I am seeing myself as a business person.

7. I am seeing myself as a manager.

8. I am seeing myself in a fulfilling relationship.

9. I am seeing myself in clothes that reflect my success

> *"Most of the things worth doing in the world had been declared impossible before they were attempted."*
> – EARL NIGHTINGALE

FIFTEEN STEPS TO STRENGTHENING YOUR COPING SKILLS
Here are some steps you can take to build up resilience, strengthen your coping skills, and make adversity work for you:
1. Practice failing. Look for opportunities to put yourself in difficult situations where you might fall flat on your face. Resiliency develops when we acknowledge our weaknesses and flaws. If you are in an environment where nothing challenging happens, you won't have the motivation to learn how to bounce back.

2. Take small risks. Don't allow the fear of failure to keep you from trying something new. Seek out challenges and look for new ways of doing things. When you bounce back from the small catastrophes, you will be strengthening the coping skills to rebound from the big ones.

3. Shake off the victim stance. Give yourself a set amount of time to feel sorry for yourself or grieve a loss, then move on. When you are invited to a "poor me" personal pity-party, you can agree to show up, but don't stay long. Instead of moaning, "What a loser I am!" or "Everything happens to me," tell yourself that just because you are a failure now doesn't mean you are a failure. Don't take it personally and refuse to let it define who you are.

4. Check your explanatory style. The way you explain problems, glitches, complications, and the world around you affects your adaptability. Optimists have the ability to attribute difficulties to transitory, non-permanent conditions rather than to personal inadequacies, enduring weaknesses, or inherent flaws. They recognize that everything is temporary and nothing is permanent. To them, it was simply a demanding customer or a computer glitch or a bad-hair day. Pessimists, on the other hand, think it's a lasting condition and assume personal responsibility for every failure. Even when they achieve success, they see it as sheer luck, a fluke, or a coincidence.

5. Regain your perspective. You'll have a better chance at bouncing back if you can step away from the situation and get a view of the bigger picture. Detach yourself and ask what this will mean to you in five or ten years. Positive reframing will give you a fresh perspective with which to evaluate what has happened to you and decide whether it is worth losing inner peace over it.

6. Become flexible. Do you remember Gumby, the little animated green-clay character? You may have watched his adventures with Pokey and the gang on television. Well, the thing about Gumby is that he is so bendable and pliable. This little guy is as supple as you can get. He can be stretched all out of shape and then spring right back into form again. Does that sound like you? If you don't have some flexibility or know how to give a little when you're stretched, you will eventually break in two. Being rigid causes you to crack when difficulties and hardships strike.

7. Quit recycling old emotions. You can easily get caught in the rut of developing one long, drawn-out excuse for why you still have problems years later. We could all find a reason to be the way we are; however, none of us have a valid reason to stay that way.

8. Make the best of the worst. People who bounce back from past setbacks and move confidently into the future believe that what-ever the problem, they will make something good come from it. At a large corporation where I presented one of my workshops, employees Deanna and Shelly were both notified that their com-pany was downsizing. They knew they would lose their jobs. Shelley's first thought was, "This is the worst thing that could ever happen to me. I can't see myself ever pulling through." Deanna, although initially devastated, eventually came to the place where she thought, I've always wondered what it would be like to turn my hobby into a business. Now it looks like I'm going to have the chance. Decide to first assess the new reality and then look for innovative ways to adapt.

9. Learn to curb your emotions and keep them in check. Most of us react emotionally to a major crisis, or even a minor setback. Feelings of anger, sadness, anxiety, or fear are appropriate and normal. But people who recover from misfortune don't wallow in

those emotions. In the face of conflict or crisis, resilient people exercise self-control. They don't ride out feelings of intense anger and anxiety. They also don't lash out and burn bridges; rather, they maintain relationships and keep doors open. Women who focus too much on their feelings about a situation do not cope well with life's challenges.

10. Develop a flexible thinking style. Being able to recognize the opportunities within a setback takes a special kind of open-mindedness. All of us have a unique thinking style, our own way of processing information that shapes and defines our perceptions. The problem is that our perceptions, especially during adversity, are often inaccurate. Whether true or false, our thoughts and perceptions drive our emotions and behaviors. Work to get out of your habitual ways of thinking and be flexible.

11. Choose to be positive. People who consistently make the best out of difficult circumstances tend to be optimistic. No matter how bad things get, they are usually able to say, "Bad things aren't going to be bad forever." Rigid people tend to believe things will never change. Survivors imagine possibilities that are not anywhere in sight right now. They can envision a way out of a dead-end job or an abusive relationship. They tend to believe, "If anyone can do it, why not me?"

12. Find the humor. A sense of humor is a wonderful coping device and a main ingredient in resiliency. Seeing things from a funny standpoint helps you have some emotional distance and view the situation from a new perspective. Lighten up and have a good laugh at yourself while you're at it. (By the way, if you haven't laughed at yourself lately, somebody else probably has!) People who can laugh at themselves and their mistakes will never cease to be amused! You'll be healthier for it, too. The Bible says, "*A*

merry heart doeth good like a medicine. " (PROVERBS 17:22 KJV).

13. Build a strong support network. Be brave enough to seek help and encouragement from others. Although I always felt that self-sufficiency went hand in hand with being resilient, it wasn't until I began reaching out to others for positive support that I gained the strength to recover and the courage to make constructive changes. Look for family members, friends, other survivors, or a support group where people are trustworthy, available, and willing to rally round you in your darkest hours. They can pray for you and with you, coach you through your experience. Your support group can also be thee to celebrate in your recovery. An old Irish proverb states, "It is in the shelter of each other that people live."

14. Rely on faith, not fate. Trust in God to bring you through. Your life is in His hands and is not dependent on fate, chance, or coincidences. When you believe in fate, you are trusting outside circumstances and external influences. Instead, believe in "divine intervention" and watch for miracles to happen. My own personal transformation happened when I first became aware that we are not human beings trying to discover our spirituality, but rather we are spiritual beings having a human experience here on earth. Life's challenges have a way of bringing us face-to-face with our Creator and the realization that there is a divine plan for our lives: *"The God of all grace, who called you to his eternal glory in Christ, after you have suffered a little while, will himself restore you and make you strong, firm and steadfast."* (1 PETER 5:10).

15. Be a giver. Get involved in a worthy cause. The Bible says, *"Let us not love with words or tongue but with actions and in truth."* (1 JOHN 3:18). See where you can volunteer your time, talents and energy.

Resiliency comes from finding ways to make a valuable contribution. The more you get connected to the bigger things in life, beyond yourself, the more pliable you will be. Being involved with your church, community, or a larger cause helps put your personal problems into perspective. People who live self-absorbed, "me-centered" lives have greater difficulty finding meaning in their life and don't weather trauma as well. Lucy Lucom says "If the world seems cold to you, kindle fires to warm it."

1. Accept yourself. Stop being your own worst critic. Stand in front of a mirror, pat yourself on the back and congratulate yourself for the good things you did today. Be your own best friend.

2. Seize your dreams. List your 10 most cherished dreams, and do one thing today to help make the first one a reality. Do something tomorrow towards realizing the second and continue down the list.

3. Seize the year. Tell yourself this year is going to be my year. Write 10 things you will accomplish in the new year and place the list where you will see it every day.

4. Seize the day. Write down each morning, in priority order, ten things you will accomplish that day. Start at the top, and check off each task as it is completed.

5. Take control of your career. Ask yourself, Dennis Kimbro says, what job or career would give you so much personal satisfaction that you would do it for free. Make a move right now- check the help wanted ad or fill out an employment or college application. Search the internet.

6. Make a personal budget, and start saving at least 10 percent of your monthly earnings.

7. Improve your love life if you are married or otherwise attached. Re-evaluate the relationship. Is it missing something? Is there something you're not getting from it? Or something you're not giving to it? Identify the problem and the opportunity for change. Then discuss with your partner what's needed and commit to make the change today. Improve your love life if you are single and looking for Ms. Right or Mr. Right. Make a game plan. Re-evaluate yourself Look for ways to accentuate your attractiveness. Circulate in groups where you would most likely find the man or woman of your dreams. And when you find him or her, swallow your pride, overcome your shyness and ask for a date. If you ask, you will lose sometimes. If you don't ask, you will lose all of the time.

8. Improve your mind. Turn off the TV and pick up a book. Attend a lecture or interesting play. Enroll in a class or classes at a local college or business school.

9. Improve your body. After consulting your doctor, create a personal exercise routine. Exercise by walking, jogging, swimming or bicycling.

10. Improve your body —Adopt a nutritious diet plan and stick-to-it. Seek professional help, if necessary.

11. Improve your appearance. Get a new hairdo, dress or suit. Treat yourself to a relaxing body massage or a hot sauna.

12. Work on your interpersonal relationships. Open up the lines of

communication with co-workers, friends and loved ones. If an old misunderstanding is complicating your life, resolve to resolve the conflict with the person involved. Drop it, talk it out or get out of the relationship.

13. Avoid negative people and negative thoughts. It's in your best interest to get rid of negative "friends." You don't need people in your life who make you feel bad by putting you down. And self-talk like "I cannot, I should not, I must not" keep you from getting what you want. Negative thoughts can make you sick.

14. Renew and deepen your spiritual faith. Meditate on the mysteries and wonder of life. Commit yourself and have faith in something bigger than your personal striving.

15. Stop procrastinating. Reread numbers 1 through 14 above. Make a commitment to follow through. Regularly review your progress throughout the year. Do it today. Do it now!

Affirmations

Affirmations are short statements that, when repeated in a consistent manner, promote coping. When confronted by an unexpected event, use the affirmation "*I can handle it,*" while breathing in. When experiencing moments of anxiety, anger or tenseness, use the affirmation "*I am relaxed.*" Think "I am" while breathing in and "relaxed" while breathing out.

If you are a spiritual person, recite bible quotations such as the one below to release a stress build up or tension from your body.

"He will take care of his flock like a shepherd;
he will gather the lambs together and carry them in his arms;
he will gently lead their mothers." – CHRONICLES 40:11

Affirm:

Today I refuse to worry about old wrongs.
Yesterday ended at midnight.
– DOLLY SEWELL, Nottingham, England

DEVELOP YOUR SELF-ESTEEM FOR BUSINESS SUCCESS
To help you discover the unconscious barriers that may be blocking your success, examine your beliefs and attitudes about money and success. Do you see money as "the root of all evil?" How do you feel about wealthy people or people with money? Are they people you like and admire? If you dislike wealthy people, you will never allow yourself to become wealthy, especially if you like yourself now. For you would have to dislike yourself to become one of the wealthy.

Do the exercises below to help you gain freedom from feelings of low self-worth, and an undeserving mental program. What can you do to improve the aspects of your personality? State what you will do to create a new you.

1. **My New Self-Esteem:**
   a. Self-Concept/Identity

   b. Self-Worth

   c. Self-Respect

2. **My New Self-Image:**
   a. My strengths are:

   b. The way I appear to others is:

   c. The handicap/s I have to overcome are

94

3. **My New Self-Acceptance/Appreciation:**
   a. I like myself, even though I have faults.

4. **Say to yourself: My New Self-Confidence is I Am Capable and Competent.**

5. **My New Communication Skills Are:**

6. Listed below are general character traits needed for success in a business.
   Where do you fall on a scale of 1-10 in personal development in these areas? 1 the highest level of proficiency, and 10 the lowest.

   a. Responsible – I am responsible because _____
   _____

   b. Dependable – I am dependable because _____
   _____

   c. Trustworthy – I am trustworthy because _____
   _____

   d. Accountable – I am accountable because _____
   _____

Chapter 9

SECRETS OF SUCCESS

Success is whatever you want it to be. It is your ability to dream or imagine something in your mind and create that in the physical realm; from the ethers to the real world. Success is any dream, desire, goals you long for and eventually achieve. Your desires may be personal, professional, spiritual or a combination of all you desire. We are by nature, goal seeking, goal striving individuals. If we are not seeking ways to improve ourselves on a personal, professional and spiritual level, decay of the mind sets in, and we begin to die slowly.

It is the nature of the human species to evolve, improve, and perfect its flaws or deficiencies. When this does not happen stagnation occurs in our physiological system, in the form of disease, slow degeneration and cell destruction until all the cells in our body no longer gives off energy or light. We then return to our original form of dust, "ashes to ashes and dust to dust."

The natural progression of the human species is birth → goal seeker/goal striving → movement → energy → excitement → enthusiasm → aliveness → light → contentment → love → joy → bliss → peace with oneself, one's God and all species on planet earth → end of reincarnation → eternal life. The unnatural progression of the human species is birth, unhealthy living of anger, hostility, chemical/substance/emotional/physical abuse, fear, low self-worth, low self-esteem, lack of confidence, lack of money, limitation of all form, lack of faith in God, Supreme Being/isolation/aloneness/no spiritual support, confusion →lack of trust in others → disorganization →destruction → apathy → emotional death → physiological death → dis-

96

integration → reincarnation to learn unlearned lessons to end our birth to death cycle of life.

There are many secrets of Success. I will focus on some of the principle. However, the key concept I want you to remember is that we are endowed with all the traits and attributes of God, therefore we manifest instantly everything we think and feel. We are thinking, feeling manifesting human machines. We create our world with our thoughts. Therefore, you have invented the world you live from and experience every day. We can manifest joy, love, peace harmony, and wealth or we can manifest the opposite, what are you manifesting?

Secrets of Success and The law of attraction

The law of attraction states that you will attract into your life "whether wanted or unwanted", whatever you give your energy, focus, and attention.

You are constantly giving off vibrations of energy when you think and feel. These vibrations can be picked up and received by other people. That's why people say, "he has good vibes," or "he gives off bad vibes." You are constantly giving off energy vibrations.

If you're feeling excited, enthusiastic, passionate, happy, joyful, loving, appreciative, abundant, prosperous, relaxed and peaceful, you are giving off positive vibrations.

If you are feeling bored, anxious, worried, confused, sad, lonely, hurt, angry, resentful, guilty, disappointed, frustrated, overwhelmed, stressed out, or depressed, then you are giving off negative vibrations.

The law of attraction states that the **universe responds to whatever you are demonstrating** by giving you more of whatever you are vibrating. It doesn't care whether it is good for you or not; it simply responds to your body's energy vibration.

The problem is that most of the time, **you are not aware of what vibration you are sending.** You are simply responding to things outside of you — current events, the news, how people treat you, the stock market, how much money you are making, how your children are doing in school, whether or not your favorite sports team wins. You do not stop to think whether your feeling is positive or negative. You might consider checking your feelings and to notice your bodily reactions in the future. We are always sending a verbal or non verbal messages to others.

When you are simply responding **unconsciously** to what happens around you, you tend to stay "stuck" in your current condition. This is why most people's lives never seem to change very much. They get stuck in a repeating cycle of recreating the same reality over and over by the vibration they are sending out.

It works like this... First you observe what you currently have and are currently receiving in your life. You call this your "reality." You respond to what you observe with a feeling, positive or negative, which then gives off that vibration to the universe. The law of attraction then responds to this vibration and brings you more of what you are vibrating. This keeps the cycle going over and over, until you choose to change it through the exertion of your will. You can be a victim of poverty due your lack of awareness of the law of attraction.

The Process of Intentional Creation

It is possible to get out of this vicious cycle and create what you want instead of continually recreating what you already have. It is a simple three step process that you can begin immediately.

Step 1: Identify what you truly desire and eliminate the negative

Step 2: Raise your vibration level. Identify what makes you feel good and do more of it, then learn not to tolerate your negative feelings. **Affirmations are an important component in raising your vibrational level to what it is you want.** Remember, the law of attraction responds to how you feel about what you say and how you feel about what you think.

Step 3. Release it and allow it. In this third step you release your affirmation, your vibration, and your feelings to the universe, I refer to as God to take care of your "request". then you have to abstain from entertaining any doubts about when, where, how or if it will happen. If you doubt in any way if you can or will have it, then you are not allowing it. You are pushing your desire/good away because you are sending a contradictory message; Yes I want it, God will you or can you do it?

> *Our chief want is someone who will inspire us to be*
> *what we know we could be.*
> RALPH WALDO EMERSON (1803–1882)
> American writer and activist

THE FOUR LAWS OF ATTRACTION
The Law of Attraction implies that anything is within your field of possibility if you desire it strongly, believe in it, and take action towards it. "Like attracts like. Whatever the conscious mind thinks and believes, the subconscious mind will create.

1. **The Law of Attraction**
Yes, like attracts like is the name of the game. The more often you focus on something the faster it shows up physically. The energetic

vibrations that you are constantly sending out into the world are called thoughts and feelings. They are always being reflected back by the Universe to you, producing results that show up in your experience of reality. What you send out is exactly what you attract back. This is the Universal Law of Attraction. If you send out thoughts and feelings all day long that say, "I am financially successful, I am a multi-millionaire", you will soon attract situations and people that will treat you like one. The day you actually FEEL like a multi-millionaire, you will magnetize a physical opportunity to become one.

The formula for how fast you attract what you want into your life is directly proportionate to the amount of time you can hold your attention on the experience of your desired outcome. For instance, if you are able to hold your attention on the positive thought, "I am now making $200,000 a year" and stay within this expanding thought-feeling-experience for 2 minutes instead of 1 minute, it will manifest into your life twice as fast.

Focus: Your ability to hold your focus on what you want determines the speed and intensity of your manifesting vibration. The more inner peace, calmness, and centered you are at your core, the longer you can concentrate your attention on what you want, and the faster you can attract the thing or experience you want to manifest. When there is a constant flow of positive thoughts through your mind you will manifest your desires. When you let 1000 positive thoughts flow in a row, the world around you will change before your very eyes, and you will go light years beyond whatever limitations were once generated by your mind.

2. The Law of Intention

Often our thoughts are scattered, which means we are sending a weak signal of what we want to the Universe. It is like a radio signal that jumps between several stations, causing the message to be distorted.

When you send out a strong focused intention to the Universe, the reception is loud and clear and the Universe can hear exactly what you want. With ANY clear request, the Universe will listen to and obey your every intention and thought command. Can you think of something, where you had a clear intention to get, have or be? Was anyone able to persuade you against the idea, how long did it take you to accomplish the task? Did it seem easy to keep your mind on it? If you are like most people, your mind probably wanders to many thought often during the day without your telling it to do so.

3. The Law of Celebration
When you play the victim game, you are living in an emotional dumpster; your energy vibration is weak because your mind is focusing on what you don't want. You must act as if you have already received the thing you desire. When you constantly celebrate your life as it is, you become a manifesting magnet and emit a super-high frequency. The more you embrace life as a celebration, the more powerful a manifestor you become.

4. The Law of Receptivity
By your very nature, you are a receiving machine. You have been born with sensitive receptors that are able to receive a lot of abundance from the Universe. However when you close down your receptors (desensitizing yourself) your manifesting valves shut down and the Universal Energy can only come in as a trickle. When you open yourself up and allow the Universe to support you, your vibration expands and energy flows majestically through. Then you live as though there are only blessings from the Universe for you to explore and have. You are in the flow of money, wealth and abundance, when you begin to trust the Universe. Then you will see your manifesting vibrations skyrocket. Money is an energy that can either be repelled or attracted. We have a resonance field emanating from our body that is actually measurable by science. This resonance field extends 15

feet from the body and affects the world around us. This resonance field is based on the emotional states that we walk around in. These emotional states are created by a sequence of internal **pictures, sounds and feelings** that occur in a particular pattern. The repetition of these pictures, sounds and feelings creates our emotional state, which in turn creates our resonance field.

When you can harness the power of your emotions, then you can harness your resonance field, thereby having an effect on the world around you and the things you attract or repel into your reality.

Let us look the metaphor of relationships. Did you know that you are in a relationship with money? Have you been in adult relationships that were less than successful? If we're less than successful in our relationships, what does an adult do? Do we make adjustments? Do we notice the mistakes we made and stop repeating the same errors as we proceed forward?

We learn from our experiences and we make adjustments. We also are in a relationship with money, there we have to adjust the internal money aspects of ourselves so we can become more compatible in our relationship to money.

Ninety percent of our money mindset is at the subconscious level, and ten percent is conscious. Therefore it is important to look at what's going on at the 90% level of our subconscious mind.

Understanding the Law of Attraction
Let's talk about "Trust" by Elyse Killoran
Knowing and trusting. This seems to be where many of us fall short. If we looked at the feeling of trust on a spectrum (from low to high vibration) it might look something like this:

- Fear (total lack of trust)
- Discouragement
- Worry
- Pessimism
- Neutrality
- Hopefulness
- Positive Expectation/Belief
- Trust/Faith
- Knowing/Conviction

Much as we would like to leap right into "conviction", a sustainable shift in our mindset/beliefs will only happen in conjunction with a systematic and incremental advancement as we move up the vibrational scale.

Secrets of the Wealthy

The key to wealth and riches is the training and conditioning of your mind to think and believe that you can become wealthy. Due to my poverty upbringing and life circumstances, it took me many years before I believed that I deserved wealth or could become wealthy. I know now that the key to success, wealth and richness of life is the thoughts we think every minute of the day. Our subconscious mind will always respond to a positive direction, It does not understand the reverse negative or indifferent approach. I do know that God wants us to be a success, because it requires us to tap into a power greater than ourselves and have what we desire. Many people refer to this as your Higher Power, Universal Mind, Divine Wisdom, The Power, Source, our God. You can use whatever word feel comfortable to you. Just remember that you want to link your energy vibration with a constant power and source that is unchanging that make the universe revolve on its own and keeps you and I breathing, walking, thinking and talking without effort.

The three things that cause wealth to occur in a person's life are:

Managing your cash flow

Managing your relationships

Management of yourself.

So how can we make this happen? We have to move ourselves along a continuum so that we can anchor ourselves in a space of conviction and trust? It is crucial to note that, although "hopefulness" and "positive expectation" are needed, we have to move beyond the intellectual pursuit of "positive expectation."

James Redfield, author of the "Celestine Prophesy," says "I firmly believe that this level of experience is humanity's destiny, but it is not real for any of us until we discover it individually and map it out in our own terms...In fact, it can be argued that those who take a strictly intellectual approach to money will be the last to get it."

THINGS I WILL CHANGE AS OF TODAY

I Now Affirm:

I like me! I like the person I am becoming.

I trust my judgment, and my decision making ability.

I know my mind is as good as that of another person.

My mind will work for me and I make wise decisions.

I can depend on my mind to remember things.

That I can figure things out with my keen, sharp, mind.

I can release all anger, resentment and unhappy

thought from the past to be free.

It is O.K. for me to make a mistake.

It is O.K. for me to not be perfect.

It is O.K. for me to not know everything.

It is O.K. for me to be criticized.

It is O.K. for me to relax, and be me.

It is O.K. for me to enjoy life.

WINNERS V. LOSERS

The winner is always a part of the answer;
The Loser is always a part of the problem;
The Winner always has a program;
The Loser always has an excuse;
The Winner says "Let me do It for you;"
The Loser says "That's not my job;"
The Winner sees an answer for every problem;
The Loser sees a problem for every answer;
The Winner sees a green near every sand trap;
The Loser sees two sand traps near every green;
The Winner says "It may be difficult but it's possible."
The Loser says "It may be possible, but it's too difficult."

SUCCESS NOW

Are you ready for Success Now? To be successful in any endeavor you must have sales ability. You must be able to sell the greatest commodity in the world, yourself. You will need to be a salesperson, and good sales people are not born, they are created. The following are traits of top sales people:

1.   They have above average ability and motivation to sell.
2.   They are a self starters
3.   They do or act, rather than talk.
4.   They like people
5.   They enjoy selling.

Many people in sales are uncomfortable doing detailed duties, but they are excellent at selling, because of their people and communication skills. To be a success in life, you will need to become good at selling. All of life is about selling. You are the product you will be selling to the world. Learn to esteem yourself daily, to be a better salesperson. To help you in this area, our book Self-Esteem, The Essence of You is a good tool to have. Another tool you will need is the ability to manage money and matters related to money.

Remember that the key to success is how you communicate with others.

To communicate clearly:

1) Get in a feeling of compassion before you communicate
2) State your observations (facts only no judgments)
3) State your feelings and emotions example "I feel angry, frustrated about..."
4) State, what are your needs, come from your core values, example I need openness and honesty in my communications.
5) Say to the person to whom you are speaking what you want from them in your future communication. example "In the future I suggest you avoid using words like Always, Never etc when speaking to me, as they do not create feelings of openness or caring.

SAY YES, I CAN

You have all that the greatest of men have had;
Two arms, two hands, two legs, two eyes,
And a brain to us if you would be wise,
With this equipment they all began.
So start from the top and say, I can.
Look them over, the wise and the great,
They take their food from a common plate,
And similar knives and forks they use,
With similar laces they tie their shoes,
The world considers them brave and smart,
you are all they had when they made their start.
You can triumph and come to skill,
You can be great if you only will.
You=re well equipped for what fight you choose,
You have arms and legs and a brain to use,

An the person who has risen great deeds to do
Began, their life with no more that you.
YOU are the handicap you must face,
You are the one who must choose your place.
You must say where you want to go,
How much you will study the truth to know;
God has equipped you for life, but He
Let you decide what you want to be.
Courage must come from the soul within
The person must furnish the will to win.
So figure it out for yourself, my friend,
You were born with all that the great have had,
With your equipment they all began,
So, get hold of yourself and say, I CAN.

                                    – ANON

Secrets to Activate the Law of Attraction

In order to master the law of attraction in a practical way, you must create the conditions that will allow the truth to reveal itself to you, remember:

- **Trust your inner guidance system**
- **Trust that God/Source** has your best interests in mind and is always supporting your expansion and growth
- **Trust and honor your true desires and dreams**
- **Use focusing techniques** (such as vision boards, wish boxes, and treasure maps)
- **Release doubt and negative beliefs**
- **Create a vibration (emotional) match** to that which you want to attract into your life
- **Show gratitude** (keep a gratitude journal, and hold a ritual of gratitude)
- **There is power in forgiveness**, do it daily

- **Following your joy/bliss**
- **Use visualization or affirmation techniques** to reprogram your subconscious mind
- **Use releasing techniques** (such as The Sedona Method, or Emotional Freedom Therapy to shift deep-seated feelings)
- **Use the power of deliberate intention** and act as if you already have it.

Fear of Success, never, how could you ever achieve too much, accomplish too much, do or be too much. Most people have the opposite problem. They have not set their heights far enough. They forget to dream and imagine where they could go in their career, or who or what they could become. They see only what is in front of them today, which may be negatively impacted by yesterdays' failures. They forget to set their gaze out into the blue horizons of possibilities to where they could possibly go, do, or become. The mind needs a visual image reflected upon it through imagining or daydreaming, before it can create a plan to accomplish the things we desire.

No one has ever accomplished a goal, without first visualizing it in their mind and then mapping out a plan to reach their desired goal. Whatever you imagine and fervently desire, you can and will achieve.

Secrets of Success, I have discovered:
1. The most difficult lesson to learn in life is which bridge to use and which to let go.
2. To achieve something you have never done will require you to do something that you have never done before.
3. Life is drawing without an eraser, you have to live with the decisions you make, good or bad
4. What ever happens, happens for a reason.
5. People come into our lives for a reason or a season, so we have

to be willing to let them move into and out of our life. Nothing lasts forever.

6. Don't cry because an experience is over, give thanks and laugh because it happened

7. The person who takes your hand and touches your heart is a true friend.

8. We seldom think of what we have, but we always think about what we miss or what we lost. Look forward rather than backward

9. Enjoy each moment, life is shorter than you think, you blink your eye and either you, the thing, or people you love are gone.

10. Everyone sees how you seem to be, but only a few if any know who you really are.

11. Self reveal and trust more, it is risky but good for the soul.

12. Learn to love more and fear less.

13. Plan for tomorrow but live for today!

14. We do not need to know "how" to reach our goals, just get started and take some positive action each day

15. It is a privilege to be alive, and in a body, to make a difference in someone's life. Make a difference today.

16. Live joyfully in each moment; be passionate about everything you do, love as if your life depended on it, because it really does.

17. We do not always need to know the why to be happy.

18. Love comes and it goes. Be glad it visited you.

19. The three attitudes that help us to ascend toward heaven are forgiveness, gratitude and love.

20. I feel we are all here on earth by divine appointment, in partnership with God, as His messengers, ambassadors of goodwill, earning our angelic wings, so we can soar home once our earthly visit is over.

21. Your body is your temple, to function at its peak, daily: Eat fresh fruits and vegetables, and drink eight or more glasses of purified or alkaline water daily. Eat fish two times a week, preferably salmon (or fish supplement/omega-3 oil capsules.) Avoid or limit

your intake of refined sugar, fried foods, white flour, carbonated beverages, instead drink apple, grape, cranberry/apple juice or other pure juices. Stretch one or more times and meditate or pray (be still and listen for inner guidance, or give thanks) 15 minutes twice daily. Exercise or walk three or four times a week.

22. Treat yourself to a full body massage or facial once a month.
23. Send love daily to yourself and others in need of love.

Both success and money are cyclical. They come and go in cycles. You must remember to never panic when it seems that things are not working as you had planned. Allow the universe and God to make the necessary adjustments which will be in your best interest and that of your business. When you are having a major break through, you sometimes need a break down of your old structure, for the universe to create something new. You greatest enemy will be your fear. We go in depth about how to manage fear in our book Light the Fire Within You. However, remember that whenever you create anything new you will automatically experience a fear of the unknown.

You must have a plan of action to help allay your fears. Often a poem, some affirmations or words of inspiration can be useful to help you maintain your focus while you restructure your business or change your direction. The key is detachment. Avoid holding any-thing too close to your heart, so that you can let go to start anew, start a new venture or take your business in a new direction. You may need to relinquish negative or positive feelings. You will need to relinquish the notion that you are separate from others and relinquish your self will so that a higher power, which I call God, can point you in a new direction or set you on a new path. The following are poems to sup-port you on your journey of success.

Letting Go The Past

The past as glorious as it was can be better.

So let go the tears, old regrets and fears.

Let go the Ought to, Could have, wish I could have,

for it truly is in the past.

Let go the emotional pain, the sadness, the loneliness,

the lack of acknowledgment.

Today is a new day. It speaks to you of a new dawning.

Today is a new day of hope, possibilities, and potential.

Grab hold of that wish that desire that dream,

regardless of how small it seems.

Tuck it deep within your bosom. Let your imagination soar,

Let your spirit soar.

Life is endless. You are eternal. Move through the negativity,

the stagnation, and blockage.

It is time to move. It is time to breathe. It is time to smile.

It is time to laugh.

It is time to live. It is time to be.

Be the miracle you were destined to be.

You are good enough. Be whoever you are. Be magnificent,

Just Be, Just Be. Be...

– IDA GREENE, PH.D.

Do It!

Do It! Today is the day, Don't delay.

Do It! This hour is precious, Use it.

Do It! This thought is valuable, Hold it.

Do It! Keep your vision focused up, Keep it.

Do It! This moment is divine, Cherish it.

Do It! The future is now, Embrace it.

Do It! Someday is today, Go for it.

Do It! Greatness is your right, Own it.

Do It! You are Divine, Accept it.

111

Do It! No one is standing in your way, Move.
Do It! No one will stop you, Go.
Do It! Life is waiting for you to act, Get started.
Do It! This is the life you have been dying to have, Live it.
Do It! Wealth is your birthright, Claim it.
Do It! Action cures fear, Act now.
Do It! Love is the answer to any problem, Try it.
Do It! God wants to help you, Let go and accept help.
Do It! You are lovely, Be it.
Do It! You are special, Believe it.

— IDA GREENE, PH.D.

Some Advice from the Greats

- The first secret of success is "self trust". — EMERSON

- Always do right. It will gratify some people and astonish the rest. — MARK TWAIN

- Nothing ventured, nothing gained. — ANONYMOUS

- We all need someone else to believe in us. But belief must always be backed up by skills. One without the other will take us only half way down our success route. — ZIG ZIGLAR

- What you can do, or dream you can, begin it. Boldness has genius, power, and magic in it. — GOETHE

The greatest skills you can develop are persistence and determination to succeed in spite of the obstacles before you.

At People Skills International we work with individuals, and businesses by phone, Coaching on: Personal/Business Empowerment/Success, Motivation, Communication Skills, Business Strategies, Public Speaking Skills, Presentation Skills, Stress Management, How To Create a Marketing Plan for Your Business, How to Position Your Business/Yourself, Organizational Skills, Relationship/Love Attraction, Life/Career Balance; Executive Coaching; Career/Transition; Parenting Coaching on ADHD children; Book writing and publication. Dr. Greene is the author of 16 books, that assist people in business or personal development. Some of the books are: *Light the Fire Within You, How to be A Success In Business, Soft Power™ Negotiation Skills, Soft Power Skills, Women and Negotiation, Are You Ready For Success, Angels Among Us, Earth Angels, Self-Esteem The Essence of You, Say Goodbye to Your Smallness, Say Hello to Your Greatness, Money, How to Get It, How to Keep It, How to Improve Self-Esteem In the African American Child, How to Improve Self-Esteem In Any Child, Anger Management Skills for Children, Anger Management Skills for Men; Anger Management Skills for Women,* and *Stirring Up the African American Spirit.* CDs available are: *Money, How to Get, How To Keep It, Light The Fire Within You, Say Goodbye to Your Smallness, Say Hello to Your Greatness,* and on DVD: *Soft Power Negotiation Skills.*

We offer an annual Business/Leadership training for emerging and small businesses. You may contact Dr. Ida Greene for a free 20 minute consultation at (619) 262-9951. Always let Love be your guiding force, because Love is the only answer to every problem.

Please visit our website at www.idagreene.com, www.hellotoyourgreatness.com or contact us by e-mail at idagreene@idagreene.com.

BIBLIOGRAPHY

Daily Word, June 1998, Silent Unity, 1901 NW Blue Parkway, Unity Village, Mo 64065-0001.

Holy Bible, King James Version, Penguin Books USA Inc. 375 Hudson Street, New York, New York 10014

Kimbro, Dennis and Hill, Napoleon, *Think and Grow Rich, A Black Choice*, The Napoleon Hill Foundation, Ballantine Books, a division of Random House Inc. 1991

Posner, Mitchell J., *Executive Essentials*, New York: Avon Books, 1987.

Peale, Norman Vincent, *Plus – The Magazine of Positive Thinking*, September 1995

Science of Mind, A Philosophy, A Faith, A Way of Life. Vol. 68, NO 9, (September 1995) Science of Mind Publishing P.O. Box 75127, Los Angeles, CA 90075

Sellers, Reverend, Dr. Delia, Publisher *Abundant Living Magazine*, June 1996, P.O. Box 12525, Prescott, AZ 86304-2525

INDEX

Printed in the United States
91096LV00004B/166-213/A